THREE WAR PLAYS

Roger Howard

THREE WAR PLAYS

WHITE SEA
A BREAK IN BERLIN
PARTISANS

OBERON BOOKS
LONDON

White Sea first published by Theatre Action Press in 1989,
A Break in Berlin first published by Theatre Action Press in 1981,
Partisans first published by Actual Size Press in 1983.

First published in this collection in 2004 by Oberon Books Ltd.
(incorporating Absolute Classics)
521 Caledonian Road, London N7 9RH
Tel: 020 7607 3637 / Fax: 020 7607 3629

e-mail: oberon.books@btinternet.com
www.oberonbooks.com

A catalogue record for this book is available from the British
Library.

ISBN: 1 84002 391 0

Cover illustration: Andrzej Klimowski

Cover typography: Jeff Willis

Contents

Preface

Three plays do not necessarily make a trilogy and these three were not written, in the first place, to go together. Neither were they written to be about war as such. But as they appear here in the chronological order of the events that take place in them – from 1929 to 1982 – *White Sea, A Break in Berlin* and *Partisans* do suggest to me, more than twenty years after I wrote them, that they have a certain affinity with each other, despite the differences of their dramatic and theatrical form. What stands out to me now is that the plays all concern themselves with the effects on 'little' people – not great protagonists or world-changing leaders – of the three historical events which determined how men and women lived their lives through three generations in twentieth-century Europe, all of them outcomes of the First World War – the Russian revolution, the Second World War, and the Cold War.

Now that the world has moved on and large numbers of people have given themselves over to the everyday lunacies of a globalising market, the appeal of the great mass movements of the last century may seem to have been absurd. However, hundreds of millions of people at the time took the view that what was happening to them was painfully, and often crushingly, serious, even to the extent that they were prepared to believe, just as millions do today, with more or less conviction, in the political, military or economic force they were subject to. At the very least they accepted the need to accommodate themselves to it.

I now see that what interested me about those great events was not just what I took to be the main responsibility of the time, that of examining the justifications for taking one side or another in the political struggle between competing ideologies, though the line-up of forces did present that task as being pressing, indeed imperative. My interest was as much in something of perhaps more lasting concern. I was impressed by how the coercive force of the events themselves worked itself into everyone, left no-one out, so that even those many – though in total they were still few – who found a way to resist and say 'No' still had to formulate their response within the terms laid down for those who said 'Yes'. Those terms included killing, lies and inhumanity, as any saturation bomber knew.

When it came to writing plays referring to the events, perhaps it's not surprising that I was interested in the conditions which brought about that strange convergence, producing in people as it did a mass of contradictions inside their minds and feelings and in their actions. These three plays, I now see, lay out those conditions and explore how they operated on people in everyday life in a way that converted everyday life into a situation of extremity, so that even peace became a continuation of war by other means.

This goes for any of the characters, however much or however little they adhered themselves to the ethos ruling them, that is, whether they said 'Yes' or 'No' or something in between. The great determining forces of history may have called on them to play their allotted parts in the world spectacle, something which a person may not be wholly aware of until the regime they live under changes. But the parts they play on one hand and what they *are* (what at best they know themselves to be) on the other, are never in synchrony, let alone harmony. Yet people long for a unity between their being and their actions, consciously or unconsciously. In what they do, for good or ill, during their search for that unity, they express their individuality with whatever uniqueness it may have.

It could be said that the major events within which the action of these plays takes place were all in large part latter-day products of forces unleashed by the French revolution of 1789. That period of history seems now to have come to a close with the events in central and eastern Europe of 1989. It may be a good moment today, as governments and people bow before the new century's many-headed capitalist monolith, to recall to mind people whose lives the characters in these plays record and reflect. They were people who had no great say in anything, yet who found themselves caught up in events that demanded every day they make life-and-death decisions that struck to the heart of what humanity they had.

Roger Howard
October 2003

WHITE SEA

Characters

Members of the 'Road to Reform' Propaganda Brigade under the Cultural and Educational Section of the Office of Corrective Labour camps (White Sea – Baltic Canal division):

ANDREI ZALYGIN
thirty, worker, leader of a trade union theatre,
leader of the Brigade

TERESA KHRUNINA
twenty-five, worker, variety singer

SONYA KREMKOVA
twenty-six, teacher

SASHA ORLOV
twenty-eight, artist of the
Leningrad Aleksandrinsky Theatre

FYODOR NIKOLAYEVICH LEDERKIN
fifty, kulak

SEMYON VOLKHOV
thirty-seven, instructor,
Cultural and Educational Section

The Band:

MISHA ROM
thief, poor peasant

ZBYSHKO

KATZAPCHIK

KVASNITZKY

1: Stalin's Pipe

1929. JOSEPH STALIN has summoned NAFTALI FRENKEL. A map of Russia, the Baltic and Scandinavia is hanging on the wall. STALIN is wearing a dark, well-tailored military-style jacket. FRENKEL is wearing a leather coat and a Bolshevik peaked cap and he carries a cane. STALIN is lighting his pipe. He deliberately takes his time, making FRENKEL wait for him.

FRENKEL: Naftali Frenkel, Comrade Stalin.

STALIN: (*Indicates map with pipe.*) Rocks. Swamps. Lakes. Forests of birch and pine. That's Karelia. 'The Land where Birds don't take Fright.' (*Laughs.*) That's the place.

FRENKEL: The place?

STALIN: Either we overtake the advanced countries of Europe in ten years, or we go under. It depends on the Five-Year Plan. Without industry, what have we got? Feudalism. Eighty per cent are peasants. They make silent war on us. Look at the West – depression, unemployment. They stagnate. But we're building. (*Stabs on the surface of the map with pipe.*) Hydro-electric plants, great dams, factories. New roads, new railways. We'll join up all the big rivers, the Volga, the Don. We'll join sea with sea. Look at the White Sea. Ships from Murmansk (*Traces a line with his pipe.*) have to go to the Arctic Ocean to reach the Baltic and the Atlantic. Seven days at least. Cut a canal here (*Cuts with pipe.*) – two hundred kilometres. A great sea route. New cities will grow on its banks, new ports at its mouths. It'll bring Karelia out of log huts and peat fires, wooden churches and icon worship. More than that, it'll provide a firm base for the industrialisation of the whole of northern Russia. From nothing.

FRENKEL: From nothing?

STALIN: From people.

FRENKEL: A variety of materials…

STALIN: There's a variety at the site.

(*FRENKEL looks blank.*)

Earth, wood and stone.

FRENKEL: Wooden sluices? A wooden canal? The Panama Canal Soviet style.

STALIN: Stone's hard.

FRENKEL: You need machines to break it.

STALIN: Picks and muscle. You're in the GPU.

FRENKEL: And skilled labour?

STALIN: It's a GPU construction project. The White Sea Canal will relieve our prisons.

FRENKEL: Forced labour.

STALIN: Corrective labour. The GPU have two main categories of prisoner – counter-revolutionary and criminal. It may be because you have talent above the norm that you find yourself (*Puffs at pipe.*) in both categories, Comrade Frenkel.
(*FRENKEL bows.*)
Or because you're a Jew. (*Puffs.*) And a Turk at that. But in general it's one or the other. When they labour on the Canal, the counter-revolutionaries will learn the might of socialism. The petty thieves, embezzlers, prostitutes and hooligans will learn to become useful to the people. In twenty months, a great Canal will open up the north and a hundred thousand people will have been reforged.

FRENKEL: Twenty months. (*Plays with his cane, bending it this way and that.*) There are probably too many skilled engineers engaged in other work.

STALIN: Rather too few. They arrested the wreckers and now we need them. Men of the old outlook. Like you.
(*FRENKEL bows.*)
They wanted to restore capitalism. (*Looks closely at FRENKEL.*) Well, bring them from prison.

FRENKEL: What?

STALIN: Why did I bring you from the Solovki camp? As Chief of the Economic Section, you advanced the thesis: a prisoner is a productive worker. You set up a leather business among your fellow-prisoners, made shoes for our Party shops. The GPU noticed you, adopted you as a brother. So now the Timber King of the South will move north. Use the wreckers. *There* are your surveyors and hydrologists. Give them some paper and drawing pins, a pencil and a garden to walk in and they'll work wonders.

FRENKEL: They hate socialism.

STALIN: They hate it. But they'll learn to love it. Didn't you hate socialism?

FRENKEL: I was in timber, Comrade Stalin, but I came over to the Bolsheviks just as soon as I could.

STALIN: 1922! The New Economic Policy?

FRENKEL: I thought it was the restoration of capitalism! (*STALIN laughs first, then FRENKEL.*)

STALIN: You made a million. From logs!

FRENKEL: That's all in the past, Comrade Stalin.

STALIN: No, it's here in the present. (*Puffs at pipe.*) The Five-Year Plan is our blueprint for industrialisation. It needs men of a special stamp. Comrade Frenkel, I've selected you to manage the work at the White Sea Canal. I entrust the reforging of a hundred thousand counter-revolutionary and anti-socialist elements to you. (*Laughs. Pause.*) What are your plans?

FRENKEL: Plans?

STALIN: I hope you'll use the same methods you used at Solovki.

FRENKEL: Yes.

STALIN: A seven-day week. Bread and hot soup for shock work and overfulfilment of norms. Remission of sentence for a constant two hundred per cent above norm. You will set the norm, of course.

FRENKEL: Yes, Comrade Stalin.

STALIN: The Canal must be built in a short time, it must be built cheaply, it must be built strong.

FRENKEL: The White Sea-Baltic Canal will be built on the initiative and according to the instructions of Comrade Stalin!

(*The actor playing Stalin (ZALYGIN) puts away the pipe and takes off the moustache. He goes down to the audience.*)

ZALYGIN: The performance is over.

(*He bows to the audience. He turns away, unbuttoning his well-tailored jacket, which he takes off and neatly folds away in a case. The actor playing Frenkel (ORLOV) also changes his clothes. They both dress in their work-site rags, patched or torn shirt, faded blue cotton jacket or coat, and felt boots with holes in them.*

The stage lights up to reveal the interior of the main room of one of the workers' clubs on the Canal construction. There is a stove in one corner, with felt boots drying round it. Wooden benches, a wooden table, a wooden shelf. A microphone and transmitter are on the table. A frayed horse-hair mat is on the floor. Lenin's and Stalin's portraits hang side by side on the wall, a red star above them. A slogan on the wall (white letters on a red background) reads, 'WE WILL BUILD IT AHEAD OF TIME, CHEAPLY AND STRONG.' VOLKHOV enters hurriedly.)

VOLKHOV: Fall in, fall in!

(*ZALYGIN takes VOLKHOV's stool. VOLKHOV directs precisely where to place it, in a prominent position.*)

Something special today!

(*VOLKHOV is carrying an old leather suitcase, and a wooden box marked, 'TO THE SUPREME SOVIET. COMPLAINTS.' He puts the case safely in a corner and hangs the box prominently on a nail, while ZALYGIN bangs on a tin tray with a hammer.*)

ZALYGIN: The Road to Reform Propaganda Brigade, fall in!

(*The other members of the Propaganda Brigade emerge, including the BAND. They are all trying to get warm. Some go to the barely-warm stove. VOLKHOV pushes them to line up in the middle of the room. ZALYGIN switches on the transmitter.*)

(*At microphone.*) To all labour brigades. Fall in for evening roll call at all barracks.

(*Switches off. ROM spits. The BAND is listless but noisy, knocking into and banging as many things as possible as they emerge. They bring their instruments with them and play odd notes.*)

VOLKHOV: (*To ORLOV in passing, of his Frenkel.*) You were bitter. Watch your tongue.

ORLOV: Your Gorky is bitter.

VOLKHOV: Not in the Kremlin he isn't. (*To the Brigade.*) Comrades, I've a new one. (*They quieten. To someone off.*) Come on, come on, come on.

2: How Do You Make A Wheelbarrow?

November 1931. Early evening. It is cold and damp. The scene continues from Scene 1. Enter TERESA KHRUNINA.

VOLKHOV: Come in, comrade. I've caught a song bird, trapped in the laundry. Can you use her, Zalygin? (*Laughs.*)

ZALYGIN: (*Gazes at her.*) Welcome, comrade.
(*The tuba player blows a crude note. The BAND laugh.*)

VOLKHOV: She's not for you, Katzapchik.

KATZAPCHIK: (*Dumbly.*) Once a thief, always a thief.

VOLKHOV: I didn't say that.
(*MISHA ROM strums a mock serenade on the balalaika.*) Beautiful.

KHRUNINA: I know that tune.

VOLKHOV: See? She's a singer.

ROM: Sing, little bird. (*Strums, circles her very close, strums again.*)

VOLKHOV: Get away. (*Lashes out. ROM makes off.*)

ZALYGIN: (*To KHRUNINA.*) Where did you sing?

KHRUNINA: In Moscow. For the union.

ZALYGIN: (*Warms.*) Moscow?
(*ROM is examining a watch he has picked from KHRUNINA's pocket.*)

VOLKHOV: Give me that, you devil. Don't you know? Never display talent before genius. (*Retrieves the watch. To KHRUNINA.*) I'll keep it safe. (*Puts it in his pocket.*) If you want to know the time... (*Gestures. To BAND.*) Right, get in line, motherfuckers. (*To SONYA KREMKOVA.*) Beg your pardon, teach. Band of bleeding hooligans. (*To KHRUNINA.*) Come here, girl.
(*VOLKHOV stands KHRUNINA to one side while he introduces the members of the Brigade.*)
Leader of the Road to Reform Propaganda Brigade, Comrade Andrei Zalygin.
(*ZALYGIN bows slightly, smiles warmly.*)
Sasha Orlov, actor of the Leningrad Aleksandrinsky Theatre.

ORLOV: Artist of the Aleksandrinsky Theatre, Leningrad.

VOLKHOV: Very well. An art is as good as a fart. Artist of the Aleksandrinsky Theatre, Le... Shit your Leningrad.

ORLOV: It is a city bequeathed by the Supreme Soviet with the name of our great teacher Lenin.

VOLKHOV: Give over. Comrade Sonya Kremkova, a good and close comrade, eh Sonya? (*Laughs.*) – a real teacher, her methods being most suited to a corrective establishment of this nature. The old goat there with the white beard and prayers dropping out of his arse-hole is the esteemed, dispossessed kulak, Lederkin.

LEDERKIN: (*Prostrates himself before KHRUNINA.*) Fyodor Nikolayevich Lederkin. The Lord protect you, gracious lady. Believe in the wild birds.

KVASNITZKY: Give him a bone.

VOLKHOV: We can do without your wit, Kvasnitzky.

KVASNITZKY: (*He is deaf.*) What's that?

VOLKHOV: (*Shouts.*) Your wit's our shit. (*To all.*) Comrades, may I introduce our beautiful new singer, late of Lubyanka Prison, later still of Povenets camp laundry, just twenty-five and anxious to please, Teresa Khrunina. (*Claps, so do ROM and the BAND.*)

KHRUNINA: What about the band?

ROM: All thieves, Madame Khrukina.

KHRUNINA: Khrunina.

VOLKHOV: They don't count.

ZALYGIN: (*To KHRUNINA.*) That's Kvasnitzky.
(*KVASNITZKY scowls.*)
Katzapchik.
(*Smiles stupidly.*)
Zbyshko.
(*Grins embarrassedly.*)
And Misha Rom.
(*Strikes a romantic pose.*)

VOLKHOV: Madam. Semyon Volkhov. Instructor. (*Kisses KHRUNINA's hand.*) At your service. We are a happy Brigade. Work hard and you'll do no wrong. Any complaints, refer to me. (*Indicates the Complaints box.*) You are on an equal footing with me. I am on an equal footing with you. Am I clear? Granted I'm your instructor but even cabbage mixes with soup.

KHRUNINA: (*Laughs.*) So many names.
(*Sits, tired, on VOLKHOV'S stool. The others fall silent. VOLKHOV stares at her.*)
What's wrong?
ZALYGIN: (*Quietly.*) That's Comrade Volkhov's.
(*KHRUNINA gets up. VOLKHOV ceremoniously plants himself on the stool. The Brigade begins to settle itself down, sitting on the benches, table and floor.*)
What article?
KHRUNINA: Fifty-eight.
VOLKHOV: On my left, fifty-eighters. On my right, (*Indicates the BAND.*) thieves, murderers, riffraff – thirty-fivers to a man. (*To KHRUNINA.*) It's not paradise, madam. No-one comes here for a rest-cure. Lederkin tried but he found the waters too cold. You've got to work to show work. Our job is to elevate work conscientiousness so as to raise production. We provide the Canal with glowing examples of shock work and socialist competition. Norm over-fulfilment is our church. Increased percentages are our god. The priest of production – your humble servant. We work – tell Lederkin – and then we make theatre of it. That's to encourage others to work. We educate and we entertain. Can you swallow balls?
(*KHRUNINA doesn't answer. KATZAPCHIK guffaws.*)
I like variety. But it may not be necessary. What does the chief say? The need at present is to keep warm and clean, and exterminate lice. Yes, lice. For the present.
(*The BAND look for lice.*)
Have you had a bath? There's always the lake. The brigades are the basic form of reforging. But the Propaganda Brigade has a special duty. The others reforge through labour. Ours reforges by making people think about their labour. That's a matter of our reforging too. Naturally, we learn. What do we learn? Some of us learn a trade. Carpentry. The rest of us? Well, what are our characteristics? Zalygin there produces the plays, gets the stuff together. Misha there sings and leads the Band. Sonya recites and orders people about. (*Points to*

transmitter.) She sounds better on the radio. Orlov has style. Everyone makes up the words. If you have an idea, you put it forward. We discuss it. If it's good, we use it. If it's bad, we use it. We're not particular. Songs, poems, marches, oratorios. Our stuff goes over really well. It's well-turned metal, heavy...showing great enthusiasm. We give variety shows, concerts. We play plays – Gorky, Pogodin, Afinogenev, Gorky. We stir the Canal army to new battle, new life. Am I clear?
(*KVASNITZKY shifts in his sleep, knocks his drum, wakes with a start. Shouts.*)
Am I clear?

KVASNITZKY: You're clear, chief. (*Spits.*)

ZALYGIN: Ten years?

KHRUNINA: Yeh, ten.

VOLKHOV: Those in darkness never see the rays of the sun. Remember that, Kvasnitzky.
(*KVASNITZKY doesn't hear.*)

ROM: (*To KHRUNINA, of KVASNITZKY.*) He's too brilliant for this life.

KHRUNINA: (*To ZALYGIN.*) What's the work like?

VOLKHOV: It's not scrubbing knickers. (*To KREMKOVA.*) Sorry, teach. (*To KHRUNINA.*) Suppose I tell you it's breaking up two and a half cubic yards of granite and shifting it a hundred yards in a wheelbarrow. You wouldn't believe me. Don't listen if you don't want to know. In the USSR, who likes work has the best luck. Look at me. I slaved it at Solovetski, got me a red banner. Result? First in the line for the job on the White Sea. There must be a reason. You'll have your packet too. A hundred per cent fulfilment of norm, twenty-eight ounces of bread. A hundred and fifty per cent fulfilment of norm, thirty-two ounces of bread and hot potato soup. A hundred and fifty per cent fulfilment of norm on a hundred occasions, and a week's remission appears on the horizon like the new sun. Sixty per cent fulfilment of norm, nine and a half ounces of bread. You're not interested in that. Thirty per cent fulfilment of norm, it's the 'stable' for you. Am I clear? Well, teach, what did you do today?

KREMKOVA: I believe it was a hundred and fifty-three per cent.

VOLKHOV: You're so correct, Sonya, always correct. Zbyshko?

ZBYSHKO: The wheel comes off. I have it on in a second but I cuts my finger hammering it. I run to the boulder. Wham! Wham! My pick goes dickadick. Wham! Wham!

VOLKHOV: Cut out the theatre, what's your percentage?

ZBYSHKO: All mud around me, pools of water, I can't help slipping every time I run with the barrow.

VOLKHOV: Run! He says 'run'! Come on, how much?

ZBYSHKO: Eight hundred per cent.

VOLKHOV: Divide it by ten. You're on penalty rations.

ZBYSHKO: I run. You should have seen me run.

VOLKHOV: Zbyshko, you're not a man, you're a card index of errors. All right. 'Lie, but remember.' Zalygin. (*ZBYSHKO spits.*)

ZALYGIN: A hundred and ten.

VOLKHOV: Orlov, darling.

ORLOV: A hundred and eleven.

VOLKHOV Round it down, Orlov, round it down. Misha.

ROM: A hundred and twenty.

VOLKHOV: Katzapchik.

KATZAPCHIK: What's that? (*KATZAPCHIK is seated half asleep with his elbows on his knees.*)

VOLKOV: Don't dislocate your kneecaps, we want them in the morning. Your percentage, Katzapchik.

(*He still doesn't understand.*)

Go on, read the paper.

(*Takes the camp newspaper, 'Reforging', from his pocket and throws it to KATZAPCHIK, who opens it out and, holding it upside down, gazes at it. ROM turns it the right way up for him. Shouts.*)

Kvasnitzky.

KVASNITZKY: (*Scowls.*) A hundred and ninety. (*Shifts his crippled leg.*)

VOLKHOV: You should enter for the Olympics.

ROM: (*Hisses.*) Zbysh.

(*ZBYSHKO is looking inside the tuba.*)

VOLKHOV: Lederkin.

LEDERKIN: (*Prostrates himself before VOLKHOV.*) The Lord
  God is to be found in the wise bear, supreme wisdom in
  the love of fishes.

VOLKHOV: (*Ignores LEDERKIN. To KHRUNINA.*) You've
  got the lowdown then, dear? 'Trust your neighbour. But
  put up a fence.' What's on hand, Zalygin?

ZALYGIN: More songs for the new recruits. An ode to log
  huts and the smell of hot pitch. It ends (*Speaks.*)
  I never whine
  (*Sings.*)
  because I love the smell of Karelia.
  I love the pine
  (*BAND joins in.*)
  because it's good for my diarrhoea.

KVASNITZKY: I thought of that.
  (*KVASNITZKY looks inside the tuba, pushing ZBYSHKO
  away. Without letting VOLKHOV see, ROM tears a strip off
  KATZAPCHIK's newspaper to make a roll. For 'tobacco' he
  pulls some horse hair out of the mat.*)

VOLKHOV: (*To KVASNITZKY.*) Rotgut. It'll do for the sick
  bay. (*To ZALYGIN.*) We need something snappy. They
  need a boost after the first week. Radio stuff.

ZALYGIN: 'Water overpowers all. But man overpowers
  water.'

VOLKHOV: Good, good.

ZALYGIN: 'You can't break rocks with an amen.'

VOLKHOV: That's for you, Lederkin.

ZALYGIN: 'A kulak's spite endures till his death or yours.'

VOLKHOV: (*Laughs.*) And that!

ZALYGIN: 'It is difficult to teach what you don't know.'

VOLKHOV: Is that yours, Sonya? Yeah. Well, it's good in
  principle. Principles usually are. 'It's difficult to teach
  what you don't know.' Might give them ideas. Wreckers
  don't want to imagine they really were engineers. I like
  the sense, but not the meaning. Am I clear? (*Silence.*)
  Any more?

ZALYGIN: About the play. 'Stalin's Pipe.' It's all right, a
  first production for the new arrivals. But some of them
  have been here more than two months already. It must…
  pale after about the tenth time they've seen it. We should

do something for them. Something about the work.
We've built the huts and dug a section. Everyone knows
what it's like, but where are the problems?
(*KVASNITZKY has taken some drink out of the tuba.*
VOLKHOV gets up. ROM hides his smoke. VOLKHOV sniffs
the drink, takes the tuba and pours the drink on the floor.)

VOLKHOV: Kvasnitzky kvass. Stinks of shit.

ZBYSHKO: It's non-alcoholic, chief.

VOLKHOV: Like my arse. Control them, Misha. I told you
felt boots don't ferment. It's a good idea, Comrade
Zalygin. (*To KHRUNINA.*) Well, madam. (*Unlocks his case,*
takes black bread from it.) Management regrets but this
evening the canteen is inoperative. (*As he distributes scraps*
of bread, to ZALYGIN.) Your Joseph Vissaryonovich needs
more universality. I keep telling you. (*Expansively.*) 'That
depends on the Five-Year Plan.' Then be particular.
'Comrade Frenkel, I have selected you… I entrust you.'
Give it a lift.

ZALYGIN: 'That depends on the Five-Year Plan. Comrade
Frenkel, I've selected you to manage the work at the
White Sea Canal. I entrust the reforging of a hundred
thousand counter-revolutionary and anti-socialist
elements to you. (*Laughs.*) What are your plans?'

VOLKHOV: Don't make me cry. (*Gives a scrap of bread to*
KREMKOVA.) Thirty-two ounces. Soup to follow. (*Comes*
to LEDERKIN.) Great is holy Russia, yet the dear sun
embraces the entire land. (*Passes on without giving him*
bread.) Boats will sail here. Huge pine trees. Rocks.
A river here,
a river there,
marshes everywhere.
Boats will sail, I tell you. Axe the trees, dynamite the
rocks. Dig, dig. (*Gives bread to KHRUNINA.*) There you
are. But tomorrow you'll have to make your own
wheelbarrow.

KHRUNINA: (*Of KREMKOVA's bread.*) That's not thirty-
two ounces.

VOLKHOV: Relax. Save your energy for the morning.
(*Distributes bread to the BAND.*) No axes? Then rock them
out. No dynamite? Right, ten thousand picks. No picks?

You've got hands. It's a battle, comrades. Do you really want to serve the people? Then walk naked at the North Pole. You don't believe me? Semyon Volkhov? Volkhov's been through it. I've held the banner. If you want to live, fight to the death. There must be a reason. (*Points to the slogan on the wall.*) What does that say? 'We will build it ahead of time, cheap and strong.' What does it say, Orlov?

ORLOV: (*Reads.*) 'We will build it ahead of time, cheaply and strong.'

VOLKHOV: A little more power. Zbyshko.

ZBYSHKO: (*Recites from memory.*) 'We will build it ahead of time, gentlemen, cheap and strong.'

VOLKHOV: There's no 'gentlemen', Zbyshko. (*To KHRUNINA.*) Comrade.

KHRUNINA: (*Reads, simply.*) 'We will build it ahead of time, cheaply and strong.'

VOLKHOV: (*To KHRUNINA.*) If you have any questions, ask Zalygin. (*Consults 'his' watch.*) Madame Kremkova. (*Hands her a paper. To the BAND.*) Get ready, boys.

KREMKOVA: You go there.
(*Pushes KHRUNINA out of the way, switches on the transmitter. A red light glows. The BAND takes up its instruments. Those who have some bread left put it in their pockets. ZALYGIN and KHRUNINA listen. VOLKHOV nods, satisfied, at his stool. ORLOV looks off, alone. LEDERKIN hums a hymn.*)

VOLKHOV: (*To LEDERKIN.*) This isn't a monastery. (*LEDERKIN falls silent.*)

KHRUNINA: (*To ZALYGIN.*) How do you make a wheelbarrow?

KREMKOVA: We're on. (*Turns a switch.*) Good evening, comrades. This is the radio station of the Cultural and Educational Section. (*Reads from paper.*) Here are today's successes. On the locks section: Dormitory Block Six, the Red Star Brigade broke all records with two hundred and ten percent. On the earth dam: Dormitory Block Seventy-two, New Land Brigade achieved two hundred per cent, despite shirking by one work-shy element. On the sluices: Dormitory Block Twenty, Bright Future

Brigade ran up a tremendous a hundred and ninety-eight per cent. Congratulations, comrades. Comrades, emulate these successes. Tomorrow, put everything into your work. The future of the Five-Year Plan depends on you. Your future depends on the Five-Year Plan. Comrades, tonight we have brought our transmitter to the worker's club of the Road to Reform Propaganda Brigade. We will bring you a programme of new songs. We hope they'll meet with your approval. But first here are some new socialist sayings.

ZALYGIN: (*Steps to microphone.*) 'Water overpowers all. But man overpowers water.'

KREMKOVA: 'You can't break rocks with an amen.'

ZALYGIN: 'A kulak's spite endures till his death or yours.'

KREMKOVA: Now the Band of the Road to Reform Brigade, led by Misha Rom. Misha will first sing for you one of his own compositions, 'A Robber's Life'.

(*ROM rises, spits, goes to microphone. BAND plays, ROM sings with appropriate looks and gestures, which VOLKHOV is too wrapped up in the tune to see.*)

ROM: A robber's life I used to lead,
a life as black as night.
To work I thought there was no need,
I robbed and killed at sight.
A life like this was sure to bring
a sentence on the new Canal.
For me it's been a second spring,
I want to live and work and sing,
The past is but a dreadful dream,
a thing I must forget.
Now tears of joy begin to stream –
mine aren't the only tears, I bet.

3: Reforging

January 1932. The club room. Early morning, before dawn. It is cold. Two wheelbarrows at back, mud-stained, home-made, with wooden discs for wheels. The BAND is playing cards, gambling for tobacco. Some of them are smoking. Neither VOLKHOV nor LEDERKIN is in the room. KREMKOVA is at the table writing a poem with the stub of a pencil. ORLOV is standing by the entrance, reading a book and occasionally looking off. He is cold.

KREMKOVA: (*Reads, quietly.*) Hooves
    have trampled
    the scruff of the earth,
    cold with centuries,
    and the brightening sky, like a sock
    with a hole in its heel,
    has been taken out of the wash
    completely clean.
    (*ZALYGIN is trying to get some life into the stove. KHRUNINA is standing near him, trying to get warm. She looks at her hands.*)
ZALYGIN: Still blisters.
    (*KHRUNINA hides her hands.*)
    Not quite like Moscow laundry. (*Pause.*) Well. What's factory life? (*Pause. As if to himself.*) Our plays always showed work. As it really was. They said, 'Where's the glory?' I said, 'It's in the suffering. The striving.' But the youngsters liked it. Apprentices, kids. They saw clearly. Got me ten years. (*Pause. To KHRUNINA.*) That's theatre. (*Pause.*) Don't you like me a little?
KHRUNINA: It's not that.
    (*VOLKHOV enters with his stool (which ZALYGIN takes and places), the Complaints box (which VOLKHOV hangs on its nail) and a sheet of paper. He briefly 'reads' the paper to himself. The BAND hide their cards and cigarettes. ORLOV closes his book.*
    ZBYSHKO takes out a newspaper and 'reads' it, holding it upside down. KATZAPCHIK opens another, holding it the right way up. ZBYSHKO turns it upside down for him.
    VOLKHOV goes to ZBYSHKO, looks at his paper, turns it the right way up. Ditto to KATZAPCHIK's paper.
    KVASNITZKY has meanwhile opened a paper and is 'reading' it the right way up. VOLKHOV looks at it – and turns it upside down.)
VOLKHOV: (*Approvingly, rubs his hands.*) So. You're studying! (*ORLOV opens his book. To KHRUNINA.*) Well, beautiful. Lovely spring morning.

KHRUNINA: Twenty degrees of frost. It'll be light in an hour. And it's January.

KREMKOVA: There's a warm fire, Comrade Volkhov.

VOLKHOV: (*Close to KREMKOVA.*) Even a cold heart makes ashes, eh teach?
(*Takes the book out of ORLOV's hands and throws it in the stove. ORLOV rushes to rescue it.*)
You're poisoning your mind.

KREMKOVA: He knows it all by heart anyway.

ORLOV: You're unkind, Sonya. It's true I've played a number of the parts...many times...but I'm not quite word perfect in Madame Arkadina.

KREMKOVA: (*Laughs.*) You'll never play her. (*Closely to VOLKHOV.*) Will there be butter tonight?

VOLKHOV: (*Quietly.*) Butter? Never heard of it. You must mean herring oil. (*Looks at her poem. Aloud.*) Beautiful poem, Madame Kremkova.
(*Tiring of 'reading', the BAND is pretending to practise on their instruments.*)

KHRUNINA: What a memory you have, Sasha.

ZALYGIN: It's what he remembers...
(*Goes to the table where VOLKHOV has put the sheet of paper. KVASNITZKY begins very loudly to beat on the drum.*)

KREMKOVA: 'Love the book – source of all knowledge' – Gorky.

ORLOV: (*To KHRUNINA, of KREMKOVA.*) I'm sure I'd remember anything she wanted me to. Even Gorky.

ZALYGIN: He's in love. (*Picks up the sheet of paper.*)

VOLKHOV: Too loud, Kvasnitzky.

KVASNITZKY: What, chief?

VOLKHOV: (*Shouts.*) Too loud.
(*KVASNITZKY quietens.*)

ZALYGIN: Listen to this.

VOLKHOV: I was going to read it.

ZALYGIN: (*Reads.*) 'Camp office to the brigades. Comrade Frenkel orders all Canal workers to increase the tempo of reforging. Before-work study-sessions this week are to consider the slogan, "Let us drown our past on the bottom of the Canal!" All instructors are to lead a discussion on the question of The Role of Labour in the Process of Correction.'

VOLKHOV: (*'Reads' over ZALYGIN's shoulder.*) 'The Role of Labour in the Progress of Construction.' That's an important question.

ZALYGIN: (*Reads.*) 'The slogan for each club room is, "A prisoner is an active participant in socialist construction."'

(*He makes a sign to KREMKOVA who takes a roll of red paper from the shelf and paints the slogan onto it in the course of the scene. She gets ORLOV's help in pinning it on the wall above or below the slogan 'WE WILL BUILD IT AHEAD OF TIME, CHEAPLY AND STRONG.'*)

ZBYSHKO: My bread!

VOLKHOV: Gather round, comrades.

ZBYSHKO: Where's my bread?

VOLKHOV: Let's review our task.

ZBYSHKO: I had two ounces left.

VOLKHOV: (*Holds up the sheet of paper.*) The instructions are no doubt crucial.

ZBYSHKO: It was in my pocket.

VOLKHOV: They come at an opportune moment, I'm sure. There must be a reason. Where's Lederkin?

ZALYGIN: Lederkin?

ORLOV: (*Calls.*) Fyodor Nikolayevich!

ZALYGIN: (*Shouts.*) Lederkin!

(*They search. They find him in a corner under a tarpaulin. He is munching. ZBYSHKO grabs him, opens his fists, goes through his pockets, finds nothing, opens his mouth, tries to pick out some bread, fails, slaps his face. Some of the bread flies from LEDERKIN's mouth. LEDERKIN rushes to pick it up but ZBYSHKO gets to it first, retrieves it, examines it, 'dries' it on his coat, weighs it in his hand.*)

ZBYSHKO: A fucking quarter. (*Puts it in his pocket, advances on LEDERKIN.*)

(*Joined by KATZAPCHIK and KVASNITZKY, ZBYSHKO beats and kicks LEDERKIN to the ground, where they continue to beat him.*)

VOLKHOV: Get off. (*Pretends to separate them but actually kicks LEDERKIN.*) Get off. Fuck your mother, would you? Get off, you devils. Think you can do anything here, do you? Just because he's a kulak. I'll show you. Get off.

(With ZALYGIN intervening, VOLKHOV stops the fight, which in any case ZBYSHKO has had enough of. LEDERKIN lies moaning. To everyone.)

Come here.

(All except LEDERKIN gather at the table.)

Sit down.

(ZBYSHKO spits. They sit at and around the table, some on the floor, VOLKHOV on his stool which ZALYGIN places for him.)

The instructions are opportune, no doubt about it. You know the policy. Labour, don't belabour. Never persuade with sticks. If I told... Do you want the 'stable' – a week on water? Or a shot in the back of the head? You're going the right way about it.

ZALYGIN: We don't need to. Any of us.

VOLKHOV: Well spoken. We don't need to. Look at me. My life's been one long drama of suffering. Beats Gorky hands down. Get him.

(ZALYGIN and ORLOV pick LEDERKIN up and prop him, seated, against the wall.)

LEDERKIN: The white fish is indeed Truth, the grey fish is indeed Injustice. Truth rose to the sky, sought Christ Himself, our Heavenly Tsar.

ZBYSHKO: Stuff your fish, kulak.

VOLKHOV: He is a kulak, but let him pray to fish. If Fyodor Nikolayevich fancies his luck with bears and wild geese, that's fine with me. The old man's wandering. What does it matter? He'll never learn. That's not what he's here for. He's come here for us. He's really devoted to us, wants nothing better, just teach us a lesson. Look at him. What is he? He's a nothing. A complete negative example. A former person. On the way out, with the rest of his like.

ROM: Not like us, chief.

VOLKHOV: Not like us, Misha. That's right. Look at me. Wasn't I in Solovetsky? And not to pray neither. After a few beatings Volkhov didn't want to work. A kick in the arse wasn't my idea of an incentive. One day I'd just raised my foot when young Prokhorsky caught hold of it. He took me on one leg jigging all the way to the camp office. 'Volkhov,' he said, 'I run the Cultural and Educational Section here and I don't include the boot in the armoury of reform. Why don't you want to work?' So saying, he gave me a kick. Well, you tell me, why didn't I want to work?

KVASNITZKY: You liked your drink.

VOLKHOV: That's a lie.

ROM: You went after women.

VOLKHOV: Women is work.

KREMKOVA: You were ignorant.

(*ORLOV laughs.*)

VOLKHOV: She's right. You can laugh, but she's right. I said to Prokhorsky, 'I'm a fool.' 'That's right,' says Prokhorsky. 'You're not a counter-revolutionary. You're a fool. We're working to make our workers' country better,' he said. 'If you work well we'll release you sooner. We'll teach you a trade. You'll become qualified.' I listened. Then he said goodbye and went away. Well, I thought to myself, if I'm a fool, he's an idiot. What's he bothering with me for? Want to make a worker out of a thief? Along comes his little lapdog. 'Chief Instructor Prokhorsky is asking for you again.' I went along. We had a talk. Over tea and biscuits.

ROM: Tea and biscuits.

VOLKHOV: I haven't told it this way before, give me a moment. 'Volkhov,' he said. 'We've founded a new state. Free of capitalists. No property owners.' 'It's interesting,' I said, 'when you say there aren't going to be any more thieves in your state. Very interesting.' 'Of course there won't be any thieves,' he says, 'there'll be no need to steal. And who'll they rob?' We talked a lot about that. Even today I can't answer that question.

ROM: 'Course you can't.

KATZAPCHIK: You're ignorant.

ZBYSHKO: She said so.

VOLKHOV: (*Looks round appealingly.*) Comrades, am I ignorant? Kvasnitzky, am I ignorant?

(*KVASNITZKY doesn't hear.*)

ROM: (*Loudly in KVASNITZKY's ear.*) Is Comrade Volkhov ignorant?

KVASNITZKY: He isn't as wise as our Wise Leader.

ROM: There you are.

VOLKHOV: What did he say?

ZALYGIN: Comrade Volkhov, the workers in our factory could all write. They read the newspapers every day. (*Reaches for a copy of Lenin off the shelf, places it before VOLKHOV on the table.*) Look.

VOLKHOV: (*Looks dejectedly at the embossed picture of Lenin on the cover.*) Vladimir Ilyich.

ZALYGIN: 'The State and Revolution.' The fact is you can't read.

VOLKHOV: (*Looks down, shamed. Quietly.*) Liquidate my illiteracy. (*Looks up. His eyes rest on KREMKOVA. Pause.*)

KREMKOVA: You already know…such long words. (*Pause. VOLKHOV rises and goes apart.*)

ZALYGIN: Let's go through it again. (*ZALYGIN takes over guiding the meeting. They settle down to a 'self-guarding', reforging session.*)

ORLOV: 'I'm sitting on a tomb-di-ay. What does it matter? Nothing matters!'

KREMKOVA: 'If only we knew, if only we knew!'

ZALYGIN: The Role of Labour in the Process of Correction.

ORLOV: Of course you must read. Take artists of the real theatre. In the old days even they learnt the parts word for word off the master. But today, we have books.

ZALYGIN: Your books got you here, Orlov.

ORLOV: They destroyed the Aleksandrinsky.

ZALYGIN: You said to them, 'Don't put on "The Days of the Turbins". It glorifies the Whites. If you want to glorify the Whites, do it properly and put on Chekhov.' That's counter-revolutionary.

ORLOV: That was the charge. 'Sasha Orlov adores Chekhov and hates the plays of today's Soviet life.' Ten years. The real Orlov no longer exists. In Leningrad, I grew in my role. When I act here I have to pretend to be free and only then play a role. I'm done for.

ZALYGIN: You're just beginning.

ORLOV: What?

KHRUNINA: The day I arrived I looked at the worksite and I thought, 'It'll wear me to the bone.' I picked up a barrow and loaded it with stones. Too near the handles, it tipped over. I loaded it again, near to the wheel. It carried the load. I pushed, it moved forward. I lifted my head. (*Pause.*) As high as my neck permitted.

ZALYGIN: When I came, I thought, 'What is this?' A Canal designed by wreckers. Costed by embezzlers. Run by people in office sentenced for offences committed in office. Escaped prisoners set to guard prisoners from escape. A hundred thousand of us and only thirty-seven armed GPU men. Escape? I thought about it. It would be easy. Slip off into the forest. Jump a train. Back to Moscow, to the factory. The same there. Attack. Shock work. Socialist competition. Fulfil the norm. Storm. Assault. There, it's textiles. Wool, clothing.

KHRUNINA: I understood my wheelbarrow, then I understood the work. Push the barrow up the bank. You see the Canal. Lying in the wilderness. Rocks, earth. Thousands of people moving in the pits, up the bank, down the bank. Moving rocks...moving earth. Terrible strength! All prisoners! I felt strong.

ZBYSHKO: (*Sings.*)

The gnats are very fat in spring.

The view from Brown Bear Hill is fine.

Smiling people take their rest –

it's sure a marvellous thing.

KATZAPCHIK: D'you know someone told me, hop over the border and there's a country where if you crack a safe there's still something in it.

KREMKOVA: Drown, Katzapchik.

KATZAPCHIK: Just give me the water, darling.

(*ZBYSHKO eats his bread.*)

VOLKHOV: You've no right to drown. Except in work, Katzapchik, except in work. What are you? An old kulak stowed away his capital in a hole and you got yourself nabbed with your nose in it. A couple of thousand roubles and you talk of drowning? I've murder to my name but, 'I struggled and fought, did I come home with naught?'

KATZAPCHIK: You got somewhere, Volkhov.

ORLOV: (*To KREMKOVA.*) I'd love to write plays.

KREMKOVA: Go on then.

ORLOV: I mean for the real theatre.

(*ZBYSHKO cries out, digs in his mouth, pulls out some bread, finds something hard in it.*)

ROM: Struck gold, Zbysh.

ZBYSHKO: Nearly broke my tooth on it. (*Holds up a tooth.*)

KATZAPCHIK: Lederkin's molar.

(*ZBYSHKO inspects LEDERKIN's teeth.*)

ROM: The kulak disarmed.

VOLKHOV: (*Laughs.*) When the wolf shows his teeth, he's not laughing.

ZBYSHKO: Want it back, old man? (*Stuffs the tooth in LEDERKIN's mouth and closes his jaws.*)

LEDERKIN: You there!

ZBYSHKO: Me?

LEDERKIN: Pilgrim!

ZBYSHKO: Not me.

LEDERKIN: You wander on this earth, Christian, and whatever you steal, you call your own.

ZBYSHKO: That's it, dad.

LEDERKIN: You robbed the Princess Apraksevna, you took her silver chalice. You killed the priest Nikitich and stole his silver chalice. You killed the priest Nikitich!

ZBYSHKO: I never.

ROM: Kulak! I worked the land but your type stole the grain. I looked hard. I saw the kulaks get rich from thieving. I copied you and became a thief. If I'm a thief, I'm a thief in your image, Christian. Ask the chief.

VOLKHOV: No, Misha. It's the other way round. Never be born the son of a priest! Anyway, not if your mother's a poor peasant. What can you do? The revolution catches up with you. You want to prove yourself. If you must kill your father, kill your father. So I killed him. I went to the Party office in the village. I said, 'I killed my dad. Out of class hatred.' It almost wasn't a crime. But young Arkhip. They shipped his dad off in no time, burnt his church and made the icons into hen coops. And Arkhip? Questions, restrictions, interrogations, exile. Just because he was his father's son. Me, I did what was called for. I've never looked back. Am I clear?

ZALYGIN: Never looked back?

VOLKHOV: Isn't that the slogan? 'Let's drown our past on the bottom of the Canal!' There must be a reason.

ZBYSHKO: Leave off bragging, Volkhov.

ROM: A hundred per cent over-fulfilment.

ZBYSHKO: Going up, going up.

VOLKHOV: I don't hold anything back. It's the last kopek that makes the rouble. I'm honest with you, comrades.

KHRUNINA: You killed your father?

ZALYGIN: He's right.

KHRUNINA: To avoid persecution!

ORLOV: Don't listen to him.

VOLKHOV: (*To ORLOV.*) There was a time when you didn't have to listen to me. Now you listen.

ZALYGIN: He might as well drown here as there.

ORLOV: Amen.

ZALYGIN: Better, in fact.

KHRUNINA: Drown here?

ORLOV: He's true to his name.

VOLKHOV: What name? I've had so many names I can't remember them all. I was born Varchik, arrested as Katnap, slaved as Shitnik. In Solovetski I fought like a wolf, so they called me Volkhov and that's stuck.

ORLOV: A player of many parts.

VOLKHOV: Yes, it's my 'art'!

ORLOV: It can't be talent.

VOLKHOV: I'll survive.

ORLOV: Just so.

VOLKHOV: If you don't want to be fucked, don't lie on the ground.

ORLOV: Even a bear can be taught to dance.

KHRUNINA: Varchik, Katnap. He's lying.

ZALYGIN: He can't remember.

ZBYSHKO: He got his red banner for a hundred and fifty per cent production of lies.

VOLKHOV: I got it for moving fifty tons of rock, Zbyshko. That's more shit than you'll move in a lifetime. As for the artist. (*To ORLOV.*) I once watched an artist paint a

picture of five thousand men building a dam. Was that
work?

ORLOV: 'I am lonely. I've no-one's love to warm me, I feel
as cold as if I were in a cellar.' (*Gets up and tries to get
warm.*)

VOLKHOV: Write my story. Make it a play. Isn't there
something to learn? I'm an example, comrades. Volkhov,
instructor of the Propaganda Brigade. How could it be
otherwise? (*Defiantly.*) Work-shy elements…must
understand how a man can be reforged.

KREMKOVA: 'A man! – that has a proud sound!'

VOLKHOV: You can laugh. I'm a glowing example, I tell
you.

ZALYGIN: Who for? The workers in Moscow Number Five
Textile Mill? They're too busy reforging themselves.

VOLKOV: For you. It's all for you, isn't it?

ZALYGIN: If it were, would we be here?

ORLOV: It is for us. Take it away and there'd be no
purpose at all.

ZALYGIN: That's too easy. Just think why they arrested
you. And why they arrested me.

ORLOV: If I knew why they arrested me, there might be a
way out. No, I'm on the slide.

ZALYGIN: Don't be so sure. You haven't started.

ORLOV: Sonya, is it true?

KREMKOVA: Let's think so. (*Points at the newly-painted
slogan.*)

ORLOV: Oh that!

ZALYGIN: We could call it 'The Road to Reform Show',
chief. Take it to the work sites. You know what they think
of us. Show our noses in the pits and the shout goes up,
'Parasites! Get to work, you lousy bloodsuckers!' The
History of a Man Reforged – the life of Comrade
Semyon Volkhov, Instructor. In Ten Easy Scenes.

ROM: Plenty of tunes right for you, chief. 'The Man of the
Iron Guard'…
(*Starts thumping it out, the BAND stir themselves, also trying
to get warm.*)

ZALYGIN: We didn't make that mistake in the union theatre.
It was the people doing the work who made the plays.

KREMKOVA: We work.

KHRUNINA: Wasn't *that* a mistake? Yeah, the apprentices acted in your shows. But all playing ministers! A Government of the Commune! What sort of sense was that?

ORLOV: Ten years' sense.

KHRUNINA: Expelled from the Party.

ZALYGIN: It could have been a way.

KHRUNINA: You were desperate.

ZALYGIN: I wasn't driven to it like you think. We worked it out together.

KHRUNINA: And the lads are doing labour. I met one of the girls in Lubyanka. Clara. No, Zoya. She didn't thank you. There's a limit to heroics.

ZALYGIN: Zoya.

KHRUNINA: You remember her! Well, she was dying.

ZALYGIN: Dying?

KHRUNINA: They said it was typhus.

ZALYGIN: She played the People's Commissar of Health.

ORLOV: You're all crazy.

ROM: (*Sings.*)
Our land, our wild Karelia,
to us we say you should come,
all you who rewarded us with it,
come, you'll remember it with joy.

KHRUNINA: Thieves took away my suitcase the day I arrived. My woollen coat, all my money. Then my watch. I'm doing time. At school, I would have done anything to have saved my father. Even this. Now I'm here, but he's dead anyway. When they crossed the border, they were heroes. Back from Hungary. The Revolution! Internationalists! They were given flowers and medals, the newspapers wrote articles about their bravery. Two years later, we were arrested. Interrogated. Were we Trotskyists? Bukharinites? Spies? A decree of the Special Council of the GPU. They were shot. On the last day, Dad said, 'You must believe in the revolution, Teresa.' But in Lubyanka I gave up believing. That was no longer enough. I had to understand.

VOLKHOV: (*Quietly.*) Well, beautiful, that's that.

ZALYGIN: (*Warns.*) Teresa.

ORLOV: It's her way of bragging.

VOLKHOV: Obviously there's no need to reforge you. You can look after yourself, thank you very much.

KHRUNINA: (*Sings.*)
Found on the street,
the body's curvaceous
(the morning papers said),
at five a.m. in a frosty gutter
and the police lorry took her for dead.

ROM: (*Warmly.*) The old songs, there they are!

ZALYGIN: Teresa.

KHRUNINA: It's still sung.

ORLOV: (*To KHRUNINA.*) There's no need to 'understand'. We're done for. We're not asking for anything. We hate you, that's all. Don't you dare come and pat me on the head. Kill me. Kill me, instead of tormenting me.

LEDERKIN: (*Sings.*)
Darling, dear daughter,
why didn't you tell me
you loved him?
I would have spared him.

ORLOV: Shut up!

VOLKHOV: (*Rises.*) It's all much clearer now. (*Goes to entrance, looks at 'his' watch. Orders sharply.*) Come on, come on, come on, it's dawn.
(*They all rise and go off in single file, the BAND playing the beat of a march, KVASNITZKY beating the bass drum softly. KHRUNINA pushes one wheelbarrow, ORLOV another. ZALYGIN carries VOLKHOV's stool, LEDERKIN goes last.*) Hurry up! No 'accidents', mind. (*As they go, he leads the shout.*) Overfulfilment of plan!

COMPANY: (*Respond, shouting.*) Overfulfilment of plan!

VOLKHOV: Expose the wreckers!

COMPANY: Expose the wreckers!

VOLKHOV: Punish hostile propaganda.!

COMPANY: Punish hostile propaganda!

VOLKHOV: Squash all kulaks' rumour-mongering!

COMPANY: Squash all kulaks' rumour-mongering!

VOLKHOV: The Five-Year Plan in four years!

COMPANY: The Five-Year Plan in four years!

VOLKHOV: We will build it ahead of time, cheap and strong!

COMPANY: We will build it ahead of time, cheap and strong!

VOLKHOV: Louder, Kvasnitzky, louder.

(KVASNITZKY beats louder on the drum, VOLKHOV gives LEDERKIN a kick. When they have all gone, VOLKHOV takes the Complaints box off the nail, quickly looks in it, turns it over, shakes it – it is still empty. He follows the others, with the box in his hand.)

4: Lederkin Refuses To Work

May 1932. The club room. It is warm but damp. There are already mosquitoes. The Brigade is off at labour but LEDERKIN has refused to work. VOLKHOV pushes him on, with ZALYGIN following. KREMKOVA follows them, but at first they don't see her. LEDERKIN falls on to his knees, bowing and kissing the floor.

VOLKHOV: We promised a hundred and fifty per cent for May Day. What did we do? A hundred and ten. It's a circus. *(To LEDERKIN.)* Kick the horse in the teeth! You're a fool. It's got longer legs than you and four of them. That's the way the kulak treats his peasants. Sucks them dry. Then kicks the horse in the teeth. Even a bedbug has to eat. Well, this is the collective's horse, do you hear? Break its shanks and you break our heads. Is it bread you want? You had the oats. What's wrong with a nosebag? *(Swipes at a mosquito.)* Don't lick the floor, it's not a plate.

LEDERKIN: *(Ignores VOLKHOV.)* Lord God. I'm a thief in the name of the Lord. Lord save me!

VOLKHOV: Spit in his face and he'll say it's dew from heaven.

LEDERKIN: We praise King David. Jonah stands in the forests. Praise to the belly of the whale. Praise the wild elk, love the love of fishes, the blueness of the sky.

VOLKHOV: You make my stomach turn.

LEDERKIN: Down with the whip! The horse has no need of it!

VOLKHOV: It wants a kick instead.

LEDERKIN: (*Addresses VOLKHOV.*) I can't work.

VOLKHOV: (*Taken aback.*) Why can't you work?

LEDERKIN: Hole in my boot.

VOLKHOV: The hole's in your brain.

LEDERKIN: It's here. (*Holds his belly.*)

VOLKHOV: What is? (*Swipes a mosquito on the back of his neck.*)

LEDERKIN: The rupture.

VOLKHOV: A rupture? On an empty stomach? I'm laughing. Get up. (*Pulls LEDERKIN up.*) Make other people do the work? Too grand, or too lazy? Doesn't matter.

LEDERKIN: It's only fools and horses that work.

VOLKHOV: The devil they do. (*LEDERKIN drops to the ground, VOLKHOV holds him up.*) Don't you think you've pestered Him enough?

LEDERKIN: There is a God. No matter what they tell you – there is a God.

(*VOLKHOV pushes LEDERKIN on to a bench, KREMKOVA runs forward and throws herself at LEDERKIN. VOLKHOV and ZALYGIN pull her off. She is crying.*)

VOLKHOV: Sonya! Get back to work.

KREMKOVA: Beat him, beat him.

VOLKHOV: I know what to do.

(*KREMKOVA sobers up.*)

KREMKOVA: I'll kill him.

VOLKHOV: (*To ZALYGIN.*) Let's have it again.

ZALYGIN: (*Begins accusation.*) Fyodor Nikolayevich...

KREMKOVA: (*Interrupts.*) No, I will. (*As if by rote.*) Fyodor Nikolayevich Lederkin, fifty years old, born Stepanidar, collectivised 1930. You went to stay with your aunt in the same village, slept in the corridor and bowed to the ground to every one who came in the house – the neighbours, chickens, dogs. You grew a beard and began to praise God. In December you set fire to the People's Hall in the village. It was night. You took off your sheepskin coat, crossed yourself, broke the window and crawled in. There was a stage in the hall. Covered in props and pieces of scenery – wooden ploughs, a balalaika, painted woods and fields. You said a prayer

and poured a can of kerosene over it all, and over the
floor, the seats, and the curtains. You threw a match on it.
The posters on the walls, about wheat strains and the
care of cabbages, burnt. The trousers and boots from the
play about the League of Nations smoked as they burnt.
The oil lamp burst. You climbed out of the window and
spent the night in the forest. It was quiet there. Snow fell.
The pine trees were dark. The peasants found your tracks
in the morning. You ran but they caught you. You were
taken to the village soviet. You were sentenced to be
shot. The sentence was commuted to ten years. That was
because you didn't cause any more trouble.

ZALYGIN: (*As if by rote.*) Sonya Kremkova. Age twenty-six.
Teacher at a village school near Kiev. Married to a
teacher. Aided kulaks to escape after the collectives were
set up. Arrested. Husband arrested. He was sent to
Solovki. You were sentenced to ten years. From Kiev you
were transferred to the White Sea Canal.

LEDERKIN: Beat me! Like my masters. Flogged six men
for not paying taxes. I was one. The Duma came. 'Let
people live as they can!' I had a farm in the war, two
horses, three yoke of oxen – two mine and one my
brother's. He joined the red partisans, got himself killed.
So I had three yoke of oxen. The Whites came. They
slaughtered my bulls and stole my horses. The Reds
came. Stole my grain. Then the Whites came again.
After them, the Germans. They burnt my farm. I hanged
myself from a beam in the church. Some fools cut me
down. The war stopped. I worked for four years. In the
stores in the village soviet. There wasn't much to do.
Then the collective farms began. They investigated me.
Took away my land. Not even the Tsar took away your
land.

ZALYGIN: We took back our land.

(*LEDERKIN looks at ZALYGIN uncomprehendingly.*)

LEDERKIN: Only before you, my Lord, my Creator. If I
knew the source of tears, I would cry, cry all day and
night. I would ask for mercy, oh my father, father Jacob,
shed tears before the Lord for the sake of your son
Joseph.

(*ZALYGIN shakes LEDERKIN by the shoulder.*)
KREMKOVA: Where will you take him?
VOLKHOV: Off he goes.
ZALYGIN: (*To LEDERKIN.*) Stop playing.
(*Enter ORLOV.*)
VOLKHOV: The 'stable'. Two weeks' special regime. He
    can pray to the mares.
ORLOV: A coat's missing.
VOLKHOV: A what?
ORLOV: A fur coat.
VOLKHOV: Where?
ORLOV: At 'Stalin's Pipe'. This morning. In the camp
    office. One of their wives.
VOLKHOV: You devils.
ZALYGIN: What? How do you know it was one of us?
VOLKHOV: You have thieves in your company, don't you?
ZALYGIN: Yes. If it's a safe, or a bank. But fur coats? In
    May. It's not their line.
ORLOV: (*Of ZALYGIN.*) Someone would love to give
    someone a fur coat.
KREMKOVA / VOLKHOV: (*Together.*) What do you mean?
    (*Outside the BAND have started practicing for 'The Road to
    Reform Show'. KHRUNINA is humming.*)
ROM: (*Off, sings.*)
    Icons and masses
    are strictly for arses,
KHRUNINA: (*Off, sings.*)
    I know no country
    where a person breathes so freely.
LEDERKIN: Along the fence, the wooden fence, two
    children are lying. Starving. 'Why are they dying?' says
    the stranger. 'Oh,' comes the reply, 'they're kulak's
    children.'
ZALYGIN: (*Furiously.*) Liar.
    (*Throws himself on LEDERKIN. VOLKHOV immediately
    pulls him off.*
    *The BAND comes together into the tune of 'The Robbers'
    Song' from Scene 5, and they emerge in column, with ROM
    singing, followed by KHRUNINA, to join ZALYGIN,
    ORLOV, KREMKOVA and VOLKHOV in moving to the*

worksite area to set up their performance of 'The Road to Reform Show'. Ahead of them ZALYGIN and KHRUNINA carry a banner (white on red) reading, 'THE BRIGADE THAT EXCELS WINS PRAISE AND RESPECT.' They set up the banner at the site. VOLKHOV sits on his stool to watch.)

5: The Brigade Performs 'The Road To Reform'

July 1932. A Canal work site. It is hot. Mosquitoes. The scene continues from Scene 4. The Brigade has set up their playing area. No make-up or costumes. The workers on the site do not stop work to watch the performance. Immediately the music of 'The Robbers' Song' ceases, ZALYGIN opens the show with an announcement.

ZALYGIN: Soldiers of the army of the White Sea-Baltic Canal! We present 'The Road to Reform'!
(*The BAND blares a flourish.*)
Comrades, you are working hard. We must prepare for a great advance. We have ten months. These are decisive weeks. Study the situation carefully. Examine your work methods. You must ensure one hundred per cent efficiency of your barrows and carts, and cheerful horses.

BAND: (*Chant.*) Never mind Elijah and Saint Nick –
pick and shovel will do the trick.

ZALYGIN: Everyone must be ready for the advance, everyone must be mobilised.

ROM: (*Clears his throat.*) Still pounding water?

KATZAPCHIK: I am.

ROM: Any dust rising?

KATZAPCHIK: No.

ROM: Keep pounding.

ZALYGIN: The food workers must provide food. The sanitary divisions must meet all sanitation requirements. The cultural and educational section must explain the tasks.

BAND: (*Chant.*) The Soviet beacon light
shines far through the night.

ZALYGIN: The fall in productivity up to now observed in the first week of every month is categorically forbidden.

ROM: They don't reap the grain, but they eat the bread.

ZALYGIN: The decisive weeks are crucial weeks. We are approaching the watershed. Every muscle, every nerve, comrades! 'We will build it ahead of time, cheaply and strong!'

COMPANY: (*Sings, as BAND play 'The Robbers' Song'.*)
We've been most free –
freely eaten dust,
freely walked in the snow barefoot,
freely were our backs lashed,
freely walked behind the plough.
Let's pray for our masters!
God's church – that was the sky.
The icons – they were the stars.
The priests – they were grey wolves
singing for our souls.
Our home was the forest,
our land was the road.
We ploughed our land at night,
we harvested without having sown,
and very gently we threshed
the landowners' little heads.

ORLOV: How much did you own?

LEDERKIN: A hundred souls.

ORLOV: What did you get from them?

LEDERKIN: A million roubles.

ORLOV: What did they do to you?

LEDERKIN: They turned me over.

ORLOV: How do they live now?

LEDERKIN: They live in clover.

ZALYGIN: Comrades, overfulfil the plan!

COMPANY: (*Shout.*) Coal! Iron! Steel!

ROM: (*Sings, as BAND plays.*)
Our pines are coal,
our rock is iron,
our pits are steel.
We build a Canal,
it's deep as coal,
as hard as iron,
as strong as steel.

ZALYGIN: (*To the worksite workers.*) All right, comrades.
Call us parasites. You know what it feels like.
(*ORLOV puts a horse's-head mask on LEDERKIN.*)
LEDERKIN: Down with the whip! The horse has no need
of it.
(*KATZAPCHIK whips LEDERKIN.*)
ROM: (*Sings, as BAND plays.*)
Glory is not in the Plan
but in its fulfilment.
(*VOLKHOV is swatting mosquitoes all over himself.*)
ZALYGIN: Do your shock work –
ORLOV: earn remission.
ZALYGIN: Work hard –
ORLOV: your family is waiting for you.
ZALYGIN: Never fear rock –
ORLOV: with the collective behind you.
KHRUNINA: (*Sings, unaccompanied.*)
Listen, listen, White Sea,
night and day beside us soldiers.
On the site are standing guards,
thirty-seven of them with arms.
We are in our thousands,
we workers!
we workers, we are many!
ZALYGIN: In winter, conquer cold –
KHRUNINA: in summer, kill flies.
ZALYGIN: If you want to eat –
KHRUNINA: work.
ZALYGIN: If you want to drink –
KHRUNINA: work.
ROM: (*Speaks.*) There was a doll –
BAND: (*Sings.*) in old Kiev –
ROM: (*Ditto.*) she loved a guy
BAND: (*Ditto.*) or two.
ROM: He said to her
BAND: I love you so
ROM: I'd never squeal. They slept that night
BAND: so very tight
ROM: and in the morning
BAND: they split the goods.

ROM: She didn't know

BAND: he'd split on her and when she stepped

ROM: out of the bed

BAND: the cops were at the door.

ROM: There was a doll

BAND: in old Kiev –

ROM: she loved a guy

BAND: or two.

ROM: Each time he squealed

BAND: she loved him more.

ROM: Each time she cried

BAND: he beat her.

ROM: So she said,

BAND: 'I'll do the work,'

ROM: and from that day

BAND: she gave him

ROM/BAND: (*Speak.*) everything!

ROM: There was a doll

BAND: in old Kiev –

ROM: she loved a guy

BAND: or two.

> (*ORLOV sits next to KREMKOVA very closely, as on a crowded bus.*)

ORLOV: Sorry.

KREMKOVA: Don't mind me.

ORLOV: Too few buses.

KREMKOVA: We have more than enough buses. Wreckers have stolen the parts.

ORLOV: I'm very comfortable. Where are you going?

KREMKOVA: The fish market.

ORLOV: The fish market? There hasn't been any fish there for months.

KREMKOVA: I sell fish there.

ORLOV: You're very fortunate. They turned me out of college. I've been looking for a job ever since.

KREMKOVA: All except slackers are fully employed.

ORLOV: D'you know, I had a letter from my aunt in the country. A glut of vegetables! Can you imagine! When did you last see a vegetable?

ROGER HOWARD

KREMKOVA: The newspapers are full of them.
ORLOV: The workers don't work hard enough. If wages
    rewarded skill, there'd be more incentive to produce.
KREMKOVA: And what happens then to equality?
ORLOV: No-one's for absolute equality!
KREMKOVA: Tell that to my maid.
ORLOV: Listen, do you know where I can buy a razor?
COMPANY: (*Shout.*) Rumour-monger!
KHRUNINA: (*Sings, unaccompanied.*)
    A pretty girl sits on a bank
    making a silken shawl –
    her work is delicate to do
    but oh the piece is much too small.
COMPANY: (*Shout.*) Wrecker!
ZBYSHKO: Comrade gangsters. Comrade hooligans.
    Comrade thieves. What I say is, all for each and each for
    all. Do the job and sail home in the sunset. Long live the
    White Sea Canal! If you want to lounge about in
    paradise –
BAND: (*Shout.*) then don't work!
ZBYSHKO: If you don't want food –
BAND: (*Shout.*) then don't work!
ZBYSHKO: If you don't want smokes –
BAND: (*Shout.*) then don't work!
ROM: Count Panin tried the thief Pugachev:
ORLOV: 'Tell us, tell us Pugachev Emilian, did you hang
    many boyars and princes?'
KVASNITZKY: 'Indeed I hanged many many thousands.
    Thank you, Count Panin, for not falling into my hands.
    Round your neck I'd place a plaited ribbon, by your
    neck I would raise you in rank, for your service you'd go
    high indeed.'
ROM: Count Panin became frightened and waved his hands.
ORLOV: 'Servants, take the thief Pugachev! Take him
    away! Lead him to Nizhnyi Novgorod. Tell of him in
    Nizhnyi, then lead him to Moscow!'
ROM: All the leaders in Moscow could not judge Pugachev!
ZALYGIN: (*Recites.*)
    We've gone and sat down
    keeping our hats on,

our feet on the table.
You don't like us
because you think we don't wash,
because suddenly we barked
Wow!
And then?
Centuries began to move.
We knocked at doors
and no-one dared say: Fuck you, get out!
Us! Us are everywhere:
in the best seats,
in the centre of the stage,
not gentle lyricists
but flaming buffoons.

Pile the rubbish,
all the rubbish in a heap,
and to the sound of songs
into the fire with it!
Who should we fear
when our 'little patch'
has become –
worlds!

We are those of whom they will sing,
'They're the lucky ones:
lived in 1917.'
And you are still muttering –
'They perished!'

Isn't yesterday crushed, like a dove
by a hundred-mile-an-hour wheel
on the high road?
(*ZALYGIN pushes LEDERKIN forward. The BAND begins
the music of the chechyotka.
ROM, or another, begins the dance of the chechyotka round
LEDERKIN. It starts with a slower beat but develops into a
rapid dance, with the feet lightly striking the ground.
LEDERKIN gives a satirical leap or two, kicking his heels
under KATZAPCHIK's whip.*)

COMPANY: (*As a chorale.*)
>Examine the horses.
>Get them into good condition.
>They are our life-blood,
>they and the people.
>Shoe them well.
>Harness them firmly.
>Whip them with care.
>(*Repeat as necessary. As the dance approaches its climax, the company, led by ZALYGIN, walk ceremonially to VOLKHOV to 'present' him with a labour award. Immediately the music stops.*)

ZALYGIN: We've examined the sanitation efficiency of kitchens, laundries and brigade headquarters, and all other links in our apparatus. The leading members of the Cultural and Educational Section have investigated the needs of the Brigade. They have inspected our work. In order to enhance sanitation fulfilment measures, they have decided to reward us for our labour with this fine fruit.
>(*He draws a cloth from an object he is holding, to reveal a white enamel spittoon. It has a red ribbon round it, with a red rosette. ZALYGIN presents it to VOLKHOV. They shake hands. VOLKHOV turns to the audience and holds the spittoon high, like a football cup. The company applauds.*)
>(*Warmly.*) The leading members point out the article constitutes the finest spittoon made in Moscow and therefore in the whole country, if not the world.
>(*Applause.*)
>Two plus two equals five – the Five-Year Plan in Four Years!
>(*Applause.*)
>For socialist competition!

COMPANY: (*At each response, they hold their fists high in pledge.*) For socialist competition!

ZALYGIN: For the construction of socialism in our country!

COMPANY: For the construction of socialism in our country!

ZALYGIN: For the General Line of our Party!

COMPANY: For the General Line of our Party!

ZALYGIN: Long live Lenin's Best Disciple – Comrade
    Stalin!
COMPANY: Long live Comrade Stalin!
    (*They all applaud.*)

6: Malicious Deceits

December 1932. The club room. Late evening. It is cold. VOLKHOV
is seated on his stool, reading the newspaper 'Reforging' with difficulty.
The Complaints box is on its nail. KREMKOVA is painting a slogan
on a roll of paper (white on red): 'RESIST THE MALICIOUS DECEITS OF
WORK-SHY ELEMENTS!' KHRUNINA is at the microphone. She is nearly
at the end of transmitting the evening bulletin.

VOLKHOV: What's this? (*Points at a word.*)
KREMKOVA: Sh! (*Peers at the paper.*) 'Competition.'
KHRUNINA: (*Reads.*) 'Think about it, comrades. The
    December norms are lower than the November ones, but
    they are still not being fulfilled. Daily figures indicate a
    danger of the failure of the December plan. And we still
    have not reached the watershed. Comrades, think about
    it. Comrade Yagoda is right. Your main obligation is to
    restore labour discipline to the July level. Put an end to
    loafing. Put an end to bragging. There's a storm coming.
    Resist the malicious deceits of work-shy elements!'
    (*Changes tone.*) Comrades of the Red Star Brigade, you
    are on latrine duty, five a.m. (*Changes tone.*) So,
    comrades, think. In the morning is a new dawn! (*Switches*
    off. Tries to get warm.)
KREMKOVA: (*Reads a word for VOLKHOV.*) 'Submission.'
VOLKHOV: (*Deliriously.*) Pure honey. You speak the
    sweetest, Sonya, you work the best.
KHRUNINA: Praise from him! What sort of a poet can it be?
KREMKOVA: Even in the crudest, poetry finds a little
    finesse.
KHRUNINA: Lie down with a dog and you wake up with
    fleas.
    (*KREMKOVA attacks KHRUNINA, scratching her face.*)
VOLKHOV: (*Ignores them, reads from paper.*) '"Too many are
    doing no useful work," reports Comrade Yagoda.'

(*KHRUNINA runs out, crying.*)

"'They brag of success with evil intent. They claim bonuses without doing extra work.'" That's stupid, not malicious. (*Reads.*) 'Comrade Yagoda says, "This is a…"'

KREMKOVA: (*Reads.*) "'Malicious deceit.'"

VOLKHOV: It's stupid and malicious. (*Inspects KREMKOVA's work on the slogan.*) Oh your hand, Sonya!

KREMKOVA: It's a hand.

VOLKHOV: (*Takes her hand.*) What it could do in better days!

KREMKOVA: These are glorious days.

VOLKHOV: The three of us. Think of it.

KREMKOVA: I've got rid of it.

VOLKHOV: Got rid of it?

KREMKOVA: Yes. (*Pause. Reconsiders.*) A miscarriage.

VOLKHOV: Good girl.

(*Enter ORLOV. He sees them close. They separate. ORLOV looks for something.*)

ORLOV: Was it eighty or ninety, Sonya?

KREMKOVA: What?

ORLOV: Konstantin speaking to Nina. You know. At the end. Eighty or ninety years he'd lived?

KREMKOVA: I've forgotten.

ORLOV: Surely you remember. 'It's not in my power to stop loving you, Nina. I feel as if I've been living for eighty years.' Or was it ninety? (*Searches for book.*)

KREMKOVA: You can't remember? You!

VOLKHOV: (*Refers to paper.*) Comrade Frenkel reports. Some horses have been stolen. And wheels. I caught sight of Frenkel yesterday inspecting the unfinished sections. Thin, medium height. Cap over his eyes. Playing with a cane. We got it right.

ORLOV: Not quite like the Aleksandrinsky of course. Comrade Volkhov, you should see Zalygin. They've been brewing vodka. (*Searches.*) No-one could have been reading it.

VOLKHOV: Vodka?

ORLOV: Tree stumps. In the dormitory block.

VOLKHOV: Vodka! (*Stands beneath the portraits of Lenin and Stalin. Gazes at them. Pledges.*) I'll give them some useful work. (*Goes.*)

ORLOV: Why do you do it?

KREMKOVA: Do what?

ORLOV: Isn't it enough for me to be here? Finished? My guts stretched from pit to pit on the wheel of a barrow. Rubbed out on rock. Aren't we suited? It can't be principles.

KREMKOVA: You disgust me with your stupid languor and the air of an aesthete and your long fingers with dirt in the nails.

ORLOV: You should have seen my nails in Leningrad. Anyway, Volkhov has no nails at all, to speak of.

KREMKOVA: You're a fool.

ORLOV: Yes, I'm a fool. And not even holy.

(KREMKOVA hangs up the slogan with the others.)

KREMKOVA: Help me then.

(ORLOV lends a hand.)

ORLOV: I admire you, Sonya.

KREMKOVA: I thought I told you to stop. *(She gets down.)*

ORLOV: Are you going?

KREMKOVA: I have to give Lederkin his oats. *(She goes.)*

ORLOV: Even doing the chief's work for him. *(Searches for his Chekhov, finds it, consults it.)* Ninety. So right. How delicately he catches that. Ninety. *(Nods.)* Yes.

(Enter KHRUNINA, her face tear-stained, hair dishevelled.)

What's up?

KHRUNINA: Nothing.

ORLOV: Looking for someone?

KHRUNINA: No.

ORLOV: Naturally, where two people share the same experience...

KHRUNINA: What?

ORLOV: Union theatres are very different from mine. They have more in common with each other.

KHRUNINA: Of course.

ORLOV: And your foundry worker? You don't give a thought to him? I'm surprised the new women still allow themselves such freedom. After all that's happened. You don't feel the pull of the conjugal tie when Zalygin has his arms around you?

KHRUNINA: What are you talking about, Sasha?

ORLOV: You have the excuse of unusual circumstances. I give you that.

KHRUNINA: Sasha, you're being an idiot.

ORLOV: What?

KHRUNINA: Don't you understand?

ORLOV: Understand! Are you going on about understanding? I understand what's straight in front of me, that's all.

KHRUNINA: That's what you don't understand.

ORLOV: What don't I understand?

KHRUNINA: That I'm in front of you.

ORLOV: What?

KHRUNINA: In the laundry, I washed fine shirts and dresses. I saw them there, but someone must wear them. Every stupid rhyme I sang at the club theatre I turned into a starched white shirt or a long evening gown.

ORLOV: What?

KHRUNINA: My Trigorin!

ORLOV: On the White Sea Canal?

KHRUNINA: (*Theatrically.*) It's all that's left!

ORLOV: You're crazy. (*He takes his book and goes hurriedly.*)

KHRUNINA: If only it was.

> (*She reads the new slogan and stands in thought. She writes something on a slip of paper and pushes it into the Complaints box. Enter ZALYGIN, with a polishing rag. He sees KHRUNINA, but pretends not to.*)

ZALYGIN: (*Drunkenly.*) Malicious deceits. I'm cold. (*Tries to get warm.*) Yagoda my darling. My thanks. All my thanks. No, just take them. (*Sees portraits of Lenin and Stalin.*) And you. Thank you. No, I mean it. Without you, I'd be nothing. With you, I'm nothing. But I was once something because of you. (*'Sees' KHRUNINA.*) Teresa! (*She is about to go.*) Don't go. Teresa. I didn't mean it. I'd never hurt you. Forgive me. (*She hesitates.*)

KHRUNINA: What are you doing here?

ZALYGIN: (*Takes newspaper, glances at it.*) Frenkel orders new inventions. To spur production on. Offers rewards. Remission of sentence, restoration of civil rights. (*Laughs.*) Any ideas, Teresa? How about a new type of wheelbarrow? With two wheels? Or a new type of horse?

All old. Old. Or a new type of leader? Eh? Wouldn't that
do it? With a new type of party? All leaders! Nothing but
leaders! What an invention that would be, eh, Teresa?
You'd come with me then, wouldn't you? You'd forgive
me then. (*He stumbles around, looking for VOLKHOV's
stool.*) I knew a man. Trofymov. Radio mechanic. He
could transmit odours. Honest he could. The strongest
odours over hundreds of miles. That's an invention,
Comrade Yagoda. (*He begins to polish a bench.*) Imagine. If
all the people let out a fart at the same time, there'd be a
mighty wind. What reward for transmitting that,
Comrade Yagoda? (*Bows to Lenin and Stalin.*) Wonderful
party. Thanks for everything. (*Stumbles, falls on to
VOLKHOV's stool, stands up like lightning.*) Let me give
you a rub. (*Rubs seat of stool. As if it protested.*) Yes, yes,
yes, that's what you ordered. 'You do some useful work,
Zalygin. Go and polish my stool.' Oh Comrade Volkhov,
you have an outstanding stool. (*Kisses seat of the stool.*)
What weight! What thrust! (*Gives it a rub.*) How could
this improve it? (*To stool.*) What profound feelings you've
seen expelled. Every time a thought strikes home,
Volkhov gives it wing. (*As he rubs.*) There it spreads in
ever-widening circles. Standard guff. Double rumble.
Triple ripple. Who cares? Each one is the work of a
master. 'Pough!' people say. 'Who did that?' Volkhov,
gives wing to a thought – 'Who smelt it, dealt it.' (*Puts
his face on the stool.*) What release it is to be expelled!
How free! I'll give you a bonus. (*Rubs stool again, harder.
To stool.*) But mind! You don't work for a bonus. You work
for socialism. Your bonus is your reward. You don't
strive for that, for its own sake. (*Stops, to KHRUNINA.*)
Come here. I'll give you a bonus.
(*KHRUNINA goes. ZALYGIN rises, not at all drunk, goes
to the Complaints box. He is just about to open it when
VOLKHOV enters, drunk, and sees him. VOLKHOV silently
walks to the stool, looks at it. Goes to the box. Takes it, opens
it, unconcernedly and mechanically turns it over and shakes
it as he goes off with it. The piece of paper flies out of it.
VOLKHOV just catches sight of it and rushes back to pick it
up just as ZALYGIN goes for it too. VOLKHOV picks it up,*

begins to read it. Finding it is only a poem, he passes it to
ZALYGIN.)

ZALYGIN: (*Reads.*)
We will wash the cities clean
in the surge of a second flood.
Slow drags the cart of years.
God's speed.
Our hearts are drums.
Look at heaven, gasping with boredom!
We have shut it out from our songs.

VOLKHOV: (*Looks at handwriting.*) Who wrote it? The
teacher bitch?

ZALYGIN: (*Smiles.*) Mayakovsky.

VOLKHOV: (*Beams.*) What a poem! (*Suspiciously.*) Did he?

7: The Inspector Requests Chekhov

*January 1933. The club room. Early evening. It is very cold: forty
degrees of frost. There is no transmitter on the table. Instead, a
broadcast is coming from loudspeakers in, and all round, the workers'
club. In the first part of the scene, all the characters show a constant
level of fatigue, which they variously struggle to overcome. Enter
ZALYGIN. He is wet, cold and tired. He takes off his felt boots and
puts them by the stove. ORLOV enters. He is too tired even to take off
his boots. He flops on to a bench, head in hands.*

RADIO: Comrades, a general storm attack is going forward.
Have you done a hundred and fifty per cent today? Well
then, we want a hundred and seventy tomorrow. The
Canal is being built on the initiative and according to
the instructions of Comrade Stalin. Comrades, it is a
matter of trust, a matter of honour. Nature we teach –
freedom we reach. The storm attack will last until the
completion of construction. Comrades, we are at the
watershed! Forget food, forget sleep.

ZALYGIN: The day shift stayed in the snow.

ORLOV: What? (*Comes across his Chekhov on the table.*)

ZALYGIN: Just dropped.

RADIO: Comrades of the Red Star Brigade, comrades of
the Bright East Brigade. You are on storm assault tonight.

Tonight and every night is a storm night. The Canal is our common cause. Only together, with our combined strength, can we conquer the Karelian rocks. Dig, dynamite, and open up the future. (*Changes tone.*) Comrades, tidy yourselves up. Clean out your dormitories. There will be an immediate inspection.

ORLOV: Who's been doing this? (*Pages have been torn out of the book.*)

ZALYGIN: Inspection. (*Gets his boots, puts them back on.*)

ORLOV: (*Furiously.*) Torn out. Six pages. Bastards!

ZALYGIN: Forty below. (*Tries to get warm.*)

(*VOLKHOV enters with the Complaints box, which he just puts down anywhere. ZALYGIN places his stool but VOLKHOV takes no notice. VOLKHOV has the speed of terror.*)

VOLKHOV: (*To ZALYGIN.*) Get the others.

(*ZALYGIN bangs the tin tray.*)

Orlov, have you got your book?

(*ORLOV looks disbelieving.*)

ZALYGIN: What is it?

VOLKHOV: Come on, come on, come on. Where are they?

ZALYGIN: Khrunina collapsed in the snow. (*Bangs harder.*)

ORLOV: Where?

ZALYGIN: On the main embankment. It's all right. (*Bangs on tray.*)

RADIO: Comrades, a general storm attack is going forward. (*As the company enters.*) Have you done a hundred and fifty per cent today? Well then, we want a hundred and seventy tomorrow.

VOLKHOV: Come on, come on, come on. Where've you been?

RADIO: The Canal is being built on the initiative and according to the instructions of Comrade Stalin.

(*KHRUNINA enters, supported by KREMKOVA. She pushes KREMKOVA away and sits at the table. She coughs. Enter ROM.*)

Comrades, it is a matter of trust, a matter of honour. Nature we teach – freedom we reach.

(*Enter the remainder of the BAND, with their instruments.*)

VOLKHOV: Lederkin?

(*ZALYGIN bangs the tray.*)

RADIO: The storm attack will last until the completion of construction. Comrades we are at the watershed! We are entering the storm of the watershed! Forget food, forget sleep.

VOLKHOV: Where's Lederkin? Come on, what are you? Loafers? Come on, you devils.

(*LEDERKIN enters last. He is weak. The brass player's lips are chapped and torn.*)

KATZAPCHIK: May your words freeze to your lips with your own spit.

VOLKHOV: Line up. (*They line up.*) Order Number One from Comrade Frenkel for a general storm attack.

ZBYSHKO: We heard.

VOLKHOV: That means you work. Slackers will be shot. No half measures in the 'stable'. A shot in the neck. Out there you'll be stiff in two minutes. Am I clear? Hard as rock. They'll blast you and grind you into concrete. Am I right, comrades? Strengthen the walls with your bones. Hold up the locks with your arms. Am I clear? Tomorrow, a hundred and seventy per cent and no argument. Comrade Stalin's orders. Personal from Comrade Volkhov, do you get me? Personal.

RADIO: Comrades, our Canal, our proletarian pride, our stronghold will be finished in four months. We are at the watershed! Storm assault! Storm assault! Increase your tempos still further. (*Changes tone.*) Comrades, there will be no radio entertainment programme from the Cultural and Educational Section tonight. Don't forget. (*Changes tone.*) tomorrow. A hundred and seventy per cent.

(*The company begins to stand easy. KHRUNINA half lies on the bench. LEDERKIN sits near the entrance, leaning against the wall. VOLKHOV whispers to ZALYGIN.*)

ROM: Evening off! Cor, aristocrats!

KATZAPCHIK: (*Gets out cards.*) Who's got some baccy?

VOLKHOV: Come here.

ROM: (*Tears page from Chekhov.*) Legs up. (*Puts his legs on table.*)

ORLOV: Comrade Rom!

ROM: If you want to feed art, you have to feed me. (*Rolls a page and eats it. Tears another for a horse-hair roll. Looks at mat.*) The horse is losing its hair in its old age, chief.

VOLKHOV: Stand up! Get back into line.

(*All except KHRUNINA and LEDERKIN do so.*)

There's to be an inspection.

BAND: Inspection?

(*They start to slick their hair, polish their instruments etc.*)

VOLKHOV: Stand still. The head of the Cultural and Educational Section of the All-Russia Office of Corrective Labour Camps is coming to inspect our propaganda work. He'll want to see your play.

ZALYGIN: 'The Road to Reform'?

VOLKHOV: He'll see that at the worksite in the morning. Tonight...he wants something special. A personal request. Lopakhin – he's a man of culture.

ORLOV: 'Swan Lake' in felt boots.

VOLKHOV: If you want to piss, Orlov, don't face the wind.

KREMKOVA: (*Sits on bench.*) 'We shall rest! We shall hear the angels. I believe it, I believe it.'

ORLOV: No. Ostrovsky. 'The Storm'! (*As Kabanov, in 'The Storm', to KREMKOVA, as his wife's corpse.*) 'You're all right now, Katya. You're all right.'

(*KREMKOVA has 'slumped'. He strokes her face.*)

'But what can I do? Dear God, I must go on living, yes, living and suffering.'

(*Falls on his 'wife's' body, sobbing. They all laugh. KHRUNINA seems to revive.*)

VOLKHOV: He's a People's Commissar.

ORLOV: Ah! 'The Lower Depths.'

KHRUNINA: (*As Natasha in 'The Lower Depths'.*) 'I'm afraid of the dark. I always imagine dead people.' (*Coughs.*)

ORLOV: (*As old Luka.*) 'It's the living ones you have to he afraid of.'

ZALYGIN: (*As Satin.*) 'A corpse hears nothing! A corpse feels nothing! Shout as much as you like! A corpse hears nothing!' (*He stops, appalled by his words. Silence.*)

VOLKHOV: Orlov. He wants 'The Cherry Orchard'. There must be a reason. Even a wheelbarrow has character.

KREMKOVA: 'The Cherry Orchard'!

ORLOV: I'm tired, Comrade Volkhov.

ZALYGIN: Can't do it.

VOLKHOV: Ten ounces of bread.

ORLOV: All of it?

ZALYGIN: Not enough players.

KHRUNINA: I can't do it.

VOLKHOV: The last act. Five ounces. In an hour. A little music.

KHRUNINA: I'm all in.

VOLKHOV: A week's remission.

ZALYGIN: What was his name? Our beloved commissar?

VOLKHOV: Lopakhin. Do you want to be shot?

ZALYGIN / ORLOV / KREMKOVA: (*Laugh.*) Lopakhin!

ZALYGIN: We can do it. Cut a little.

VOLKHOV: Cut?

ZALYGIN: With a scalpel. Dr Chekhov's orders. Lopakhin will love it.

ORLOV: What the…

ZALYGIN: Get us some costumes and we'll give you the last act.

VOLKHOV: I'm glad you've seen sense, comrades.
    (*VOLKHOV signs to ZBYSHKO to go with him. LEDERKIN blocks his way, bowed down motionless before him.*)

LEDERKIN: 'Already only a third of the land is under forest. The goats have disappeared, but there are still some elks.'

VOLKHOV: Tears, Lederkin? Moscow doesn't believe in tears.
    (*VOLKHOV kicks LEDERKIN out of the way, goes off with ZBYSHKO. ZALYGIN takes a box from the shelf and a cracked, rusty mirror. He begins to hand out make-up. The BAND begins to practice.*)

ROM: (*To BAND.*) What do you think? 'The Robbers' Song'? Renowned through all Russia. Inside and out.

ORLOV: (*Of LEDERKIN.*) See? He's putting it on. That was 'Uncle Vanya'! (*To ZALYGIN.*) If we've got to, we've got to. I'll be Lopakhin.

ZALYGIN: Lederkin will play Lopakhin.

ORLOV: Lederkin? He can't.

ZALYGIN: I'll be Trofymov. You play Gayev. Sonya –
Madame Ranyevskaya. Teresa, you can be Anya. We'll
cut out the others.
(*In turn, each uses the mirror to make up.*)
ORLOV: Dear old Firs?
ZALYGIN: You'll have to double. Anyway, we may not get
that far. The Commissar will never know. (*To them all, of
the make-up.*) Just the basic. Volkhov can be on the book.
ORLOV: (*Of LEDERKIN.*) It's impossible. He'll never
manage it.
ZALYGIN: Nonsense. It's in the blood. His father was
director of Stepanidar Serf Theatre. Under the Tsar.
ORLOV: He what?
(*The mirror has clouded over with their breath. KHRUNINA
scrapes at it.*)
KHRUNINA: It's frozen. (*Peers, scrapes.*)
(*Enter VOLKHOV, with ZBYSHKO carrying a basket of
costumes.*)
VOLKHOV: Twenty minutes. (*Feels in his pocket.*) The watch!
ZALYGIN: The book.
VOLKHOV: What, me? (*Smiles proudly.*) When he's come,
I'll tell you. (*Goes.*)
(*They gather round the basket, examining the clothes.*)
KATZAPCHIK: (*To ZBYSHKO.*) Office staff laundry? (*Picks
out a cotton shirt, holds it up to himself.*)
ROM: (*Finds a silk shift.*) Pretty typists.
KVASNITZKY: (*To ROM.*) This is for your missus. (*A fox
fur.*)
ROM: (*Finds a pair of silk panties.*) Must be foreigners here.
KATZAPCHIK: (*Holds up a Stalin-style jacket, neatly-
tailored.*) Bit above the ordinary.
ZBYSHKO: They belonged to the new arrivals.
ORLOV: What?
ZALYGIN: (*Picks up a gown.*) This one came straight from
the ball. (*Gives it to KREMKOVA.*) Teresa. (*Hands
KHRUNINA a dress.*)
KREMKOVA: Too long. (*Takes another.*)
KHRUNINA: (*Coughs, wheezes.*) Is this right for Anya?
ORLOV: It's not quite like the Aleksandrinsky.

ZALYGIN: (*Finds a suit.*) The suit of the NEP-man! Come here. Lederkin, you're in business.

LEDERKIN: I'm cold.

ZALYGIN: This'll keep you warm. (*Takes off LEDERKIN's top rags and puts on the jacket of a light suit.*) Trousers. (*LEDERKIN struggles to get into the trousers but gives up. ZALYGIN and ORLOV have both picked their own costumes. ZALYGIN has found a pair of glasses for Trofymov. They make up and the BAND practices. Once the players are dressed, they rehearse, using the book to jog their memories.*)

KHRUNINA: I don't know a line.

KREMKOVA: It's stupid.

ZALYGIN: (*To KHRUNINA.*) Sasha will carry you.

ORLOV: What are we cutting?

ZALYGIN: I'll begin. Just play it by ear. (*Gets four glasses, puts them on the tray. Starts arranging the table and benches. Puts on Trofymov's glasses. As Trofymov.*) 'I think it's time to start. The horses are at the door. Anya, my galoshes. I can't find them.' Lederkin. 'And I must be off to Kharkov.'

LEDERKIN: (*As Lopakhin.*) 'I must be off to Kharkov.'

ZALYGIN: 'I've hung around here too long.' Go on.

LEDERKIN: 'I've hung around here too long.'

ZALYGIN: 'And it's torture having no work to do.'

LEDERKIN: 'It's torture having no work to do.'

ZALYGIN: Go on.

ORLOV: He doesn't remember.

LEDERKIN: 'I can't be without work. I just don't know what to do with my hands.'

ZALYGIN: He does. He remembers it. As if it were truth. (*Enter VOLKHOV. LEDERKIN sits on a bench and remains there until and during the play.*) (*To VOLKHOV.*) Water. (*Points to glasses. VOLKHOV signs to ZBYSHKO, who takes the tray and glasses and goes with him.*) You know, Orlov. I once played to an audience of professors. Prisoners. In a camp in the forest. It was Kirshon's 'Bread'. Afterwards I met Tshirshenko. I said, 'Professor, you've just seen beggarly art, art in rags and tatters, a play about peasants, poverty, collectivisation.

And not inside, in a theatre, but out in the cold air, in a timber yard. Whatever could it mean to you?' And he said, 'I am a professor. A scientist. Yes, it's a communist play. About peasants. But for me it's not a question of what the author wants to say. It's how the audience translates the words into the language of truth. (*Pause.*) How could it be that a play by the communist Kirshon, irreproachably written, with an irreproachable line, sounded as it did to that audience, without any intention on the part of the director?'

ORLOV: (*Bitterly.*) Through the negative characters, of course. Bearers of absolute honour, even when they serve dishonour.

ZALYGIN: No, Orlov. To a peasant audience, a tragedy is a play about everyday life. In my factory, a sentimental drama becomes a comedy. And a comedy of Soviet life, drama.

ORLOV: (*Holds up Chekhov.*) This is the language of truth.

ZALYGIN: Your truth.

(*KHRUNINA coughs. ROM practices singing 'The Robbers' Song' in a low voice.*)

KREMKOVA: 'For some reason or other I'm always bored when I get married.'

(*Enter VOLKHOV, with ZBYSHKO carrying glasses with water in them.*)

ROM: (*Sings.*)
We've been most free –
freely eaten dust,
freely walked in the snow, barefoot...

VOLKHOV: He's coming. (*To ROM.*) You're not singing that. Lederkin.

(*LEDERKIN doesn't move.*)

ZALYGIN: The book.

(*ORLOV hands the book to VOLKHOV.*)

VOLKHOV: (*To ROM.*) 'The March of the Iron Men.'

ORLOV: Page three hundred and thirty.

KHRUNINA: I don't know a line.

KREMKOVA: I've never heard of anything so...

VOLKHOV: (*To ROM.*) Don't forget. (*Looks off.*)

ORLOV: 'Before the cherry orchard was sold everybody
was worried and upset, but as soon as it was all settled...'
VOLKHOV: Sh! They're here.
(*Everyone settles, ready to come on. LEDERKIN is already
seated 'on stage'. VOLKHOV comes forward, book in hand.*)
Comrades! We are honoured today with the company of
Aleksyeevich Lopakhin, Commissar of the Cultural and
Educational Section of all the camps, who is on a short
visit. Comrade, we hope you enjoy your stay. (*He claps,
the Company claps too.*) The Road to Reform Propaganda
Brigade of the Cultural and Educational Section of the
Office of Corrective Labour Camps (White Sea – Baltic
Division) has the honour...and is proud...will now...by
special request...a choice which triumphantly displays
the profound culture of Comrade Lopakhin...the
members of our excellent Brigade will now perform 'The
Cherry Orchard', Act (*Consults the book.*) Four. (*Reads.*)
'The same setting as Act One. There are no pictures on
the walls.'
ZALYGIN: (*Hisses.*) Enough.
VOLKHOV: (*Bows to audience.*) The play, comrades. (*Signs
to ROM, sits with book. The BAND strikes up.*)
BAND / COMPANY: (*Sings.*)
We've been most free –
freely eaten dust,
freely walked in the snow barefoot,
freely were our backs lashed,
freely walked behind the plough.
Let's pray for our masters!
(*VOLKHOV signs desperately to ROM, who ignores him.*)
God's church – that was the sky.
The icons – they were the stars.
(*VOLKHOV stands, beams and claps, signs to the 'audience'
to clap too.*)
The priests – they were grey wolves,
singing for our souls.
Our home was the forest,
our land was the road.
We ploughed our land at night,

we harvested without having sown,
and very gently we threshed
the landowners' little heads.
(*With VOLKHOV still clapping, ROM signs to the BAND
and the music tails off. VOLKHOV signs to ZALYGIN and
sits with the book. ZALYGIN, as Trofymov, 'comes on', followed
by ORLOV as Gayev.*)

ZALYGIN: I think it's time to start. The horses are at the
door. (*Calls.*) Anya, my galoshes. I can't find them.

KHRUNINA: (*Off.*) I can't either.

ZALYGIN: (*Whispers.*) Lederkin.

LEDERKIN: And I must be off to Kharkov. I've hung
around here too long. (*Pause.*)

ZALYGIN: (*Whispers.*) And it's torture.

LEDERKIN: It's torture having no work to do. My hands
feel limp and strange, as if they didn't belong to me.

ZALYGIN: We'll soon be gone, then you can start your
useful labours again.

LEDERKIN: You're off to Moscow, then? (*Leans forward
with his head in his hands.*)

(*'Enter' KREMKOVA as Ranyevskaya, with tray of drinks.*)

KREMKOVA: It's Dooniasha's day off. Have some
champagne.

(*KHRUNINA, as Anya, follows KREMKOVA 'on'. She takes
a drink from the tray.*)

KHRUNINA: This champagne isn't the real thing, I can
tell you.

KREMKOVA: Quiet, Anya. (*Takes a drink.*)

ZALYGIN: (*Takes a drink.*) The stoves weren't lit today. It
doesn't matter as we're going. (*Laughs.*)

ORLOV: Why are you laughing?

ZALYGIN: Because I'm feeling glad.

(*KHRUNINA sips her drink but it has turned to ice. She
empties the ice on to the floor. The others put their glasses
down without drinking.*)

KREMKOVA: The cherry orchard. It's all white. What a
frost. (*To the walls.*) Goodbye, dear house. Winter will
pass, spring will come again, you'll be pulled down. How
much these walls have seen! (*Kisses KHRUNINA ardently.*)
Are you glad?

KHRUNINA: Yes, very. Our new life is just beginning, Mama.

ORLOV: (*Brightly.*) So it is indeed. Before the cherry orchard was sold, everybody was worried and upset, but as soon as it was all settled, everybody calmed down. (*Knocks on table. They all listen.*) There! They're cutting it down. Look at Lopakhin. He had a thousand acres of poppy sown last spring and he's just made fifty thousand net profit on it. And when they were in bloom, what a picture it was! He wants to lend us money, but he's a peasant with no manners. He imagines we're stuck up because we won't take it.

ZALYGIN: My father's a worker. There's nothing in that. Humanity is advancing towards the highest truth, the greatest happiness, and I am in the lead!

ORLOV: Will you get there?

ZALYGIN: Yes. (*Pause.*) I'll get there myself, or show others the way to get there.

(*ORLOV knocks on the table. KHRUNINA feels she should speak a line, looks at VOLKHOV.*)

VOLKHOV: (*Whispers.*) It's not here.

ZALYGIN: (*Hisses.*) Lederkin.

KHRUNINA: (*To VOLKHOV.*) A line.

VOLKHOV: Pages are missing.

(*ROM puffs out cigarette smoke.*)

ZALYGIN: (*Whispers.*) Lederkin.

KHRUNINA: What are galoshes?

KREMKOVA: My nerves are better. I'm sleeping better too. In a week's time I'll be in Paris again. I can hardly believe it. Ah! Paris.

(*KHRUNINA coughs.*)

ORLOV: *Vive la France!*

KHRUNINA: You'll come back soon, Mama, quite soon, won't you?

ORLOV: So this is the end of life in this house.

ZALYGIN: Yes, life here has come to an end. (*Goes to KHRUNINA.*) Greetings to the new life.

ORLOV: Lopakhin, do you remember, last year about this time it was snowing already, but now it's quite still and sunny. It's rather cold, though. (*To KHRUNINA.*) About forty degrees of frost.

KHRUNINA: I haven't looked. Anyway, our
thermometer's broken.

ZALYGIN: Now we can start our journey.

ORLOV: (*Whispers.*) Lederkin.

ZALYGIN: Come along, ladies and gentlemen! Lopakhin!

ORLOV: Lopakhin.

(*ORLOV bends to LEDERKIN as if to take his hand and help him up. In doing so he knocks against him. LEDERKIN tips off the bench to the floor, on his side, still just as he sat, leaning forward with his head in his hands. He has frozen to death. The company stands back. Pause. ZALYGIN looks straight ahead into the audience. KHRUNINA looks at VOLKHOV.*)

VOLKHOV: (*His eyes on the commissar.*) Play on!

ZALYGIN: (*With triumph, looks at VOLKHOV, takes off 'his' glasses, to the audience.*) Without Lopakhin?

(*VOLKHOV starts to clap, but stops short at once.*)

VOLKHOV: (*To ROM, desperately.*) Music!

(*ROM slowly stubs out his cigarette, gets up, spits, raises his hand and leads the BAND off into 'The Robbers' Song'. VOLKHOV, hearing it, immediately begins to clap and beam a 'smile'. But the BAND continues playing. The COMPANY sings.*)

COMPANY: We've been most free –
freely eaten dust,
freely walked in the snow barefoot,
freely were our backs lashed,
freely walked behind the plough.
Let's pray for our masters!

8: The Assault On The Watershed

January 1933. A Canal work site. It is cold. The Brigade are squatting on the ground. VOLKHOV sits on his stool. It is a pre-work meeting. They are pledging themselves to the storm assault before an audience of Canal workers. Banners (white on red) surround the site. They read, 'SHIRKERS ARE CLASS ENEMIES!', 'AHEAD OF TIME, CHEAPLY AND STRONG!', 'ACHIEVE A DAY OF RECORDS!', 'ALL FOR THE STORM ASSAULT!', 'STRIKE HARD AND THE WHOLE PLANET WILL GASP!' Members of the Brigade hold a red banner which reads, 'CONQUERORS OF THE WATERSHED'.

ROGER HOWARD

ZALYGIN: (*Stands.*) Shock workers! The Karelian central
    executive committee and Party committee have sent us a
    banner. It will go to the best workers on the watershed.
    Comrades, it's January, it's cold, the work is bitter.
    Attack the earth! Conquer the cold! Make January into
    June! We are conducting a storm assault! An assault on
    the watershed. The best workers are here, the best
    fighters! Let's make our pledges.
    (*The Brigade applaud. ZALYGIN squats. ROM jumps up,
    tears off his cap and stuffs it in his pocket.*)
ROM: Comrade hooligans, we're filth, shirkers, thieves,
    scum that hasn't been allowed to settle but stirred up, we
    give off a stink some don't like, it makes them retch, we
    smell of gall, comrades, we're scum that's rising,
    hooligans for construction.
    (*Applause, ROM squats.*)
ZALYGIN: A hundred and fifty per cent!
COMPANY: A hundred and seventy!
ZALYGIN: A hundred and eighty per cent!
COMPANY: Two hundred!
KREMKOVA: (*Stands.*) I pledge myself. In my village,
    peasant children still learned the old ways. Bowed to the
    priest, bowed to the landowner, bowed to the kulak,
    bowed to the teacher. They bowed to me, the teacher, a
    poet. Yes. Not out of respect for poetry, love poems,
    poems about sunrise, or learning, learning about the
    polar ice-cap and Napoleon. But out of fear, fear of me,
    fear of the head teacher, fear of the village soviet, fear of
    what would happen to them if they didn't bow. When the
    collectives came I didn't understand. I didn't go along
    the Party road. I didn't bow to the will of the poor
    peasants, I thought the kulaks were victims. Comrades, I
    had a husband. I don't know where he is now. It doesn't
    matter where he is. Foma and I, together, one night, cold,
    snow, a January like this, the smell of horses, we rode to
    the house of the chairman of the village soviet and killed
    him. I bow to you. I will conquer rock, conquer the cold,
    make January into June. I bow to the will of the children.
    (*Silence. She sits. KHRUNINA stands, coughs.*)

KHRUNINA: If there's to be any bowing... I worked in a laundry. What don't I know about dirt! Let her talk. The earth'll be moved anyway, the Canal will be built. I don't make good speeches but you follow. I've never taught children, or had any, I don't know about all that. But at the laundry the comrades told me about clean linen. (*She squats, racked by coughing, but stands again.*) If it's understanding, well, I understand a few things. A father's voice. The sound of a shot. The Internationale. (*She sits. ORLOV jumps up, holding a copy of 'Reforging'. VOLKHOV signals to ROM for a song.*)

ROM: (*Sings, unaccompanied.*)
To the sea,
to our blue sea,
to our blue Baltic sea,
sailed a great ship,
a ship so finely made,
made of pearls, comrades,
and the rigging of silk.
All the sailors were admirals, admirals,
and all the passengers generals, generals,
and at the bow sat the Tsar,
sat the Tsar,
Tsar Peter the First,
and the ship sailed,
the ship sailed
to our blue Baltic sea!

ORLOV: (*Gesticulating with paper.*) Attack. Storm. Shock work. (*Quotes.*) 'Camp competition and the shock-worker movement must be tied in with the system of rewards. The principal basis of competition is material incentive. This is so in our factories. Why put camp inmates in a privileged position? Submission to discipline begins out of egotistical motives. It rises to the stage of socialist competition for the red banner.' Marvellous words. Don't bother about figures. Make the soup hot, feed the horses. But today, begin the push – the banner will come to you. Attack. Storm. Marvellous words.

ZALYGIN: (*Jumps up, furiously.*) They are for some. We accepted the Five-Year Plan, comrade workers. We're

building it with our own hands. Socialism won't drop
from heaven. No-one's going to help us. In Europe the
capitalist countries are hit by the depression. Millions
join the dole queues, there's nothing invested, nothing
being built. Won't they rise? Won't they join us? But on
one sixth of the globe a socialist world is already being
born. The earth turns in pain and joy. In this sector of
construction, the proletarian agreement is signed. Our
Brigade challenges you for the banner, comrades –
comrade carpenters, comrade stonemasons, riveters,
fitters, peasant comrades, comrade thieves, teachers, and
comrades reforged and reforging. This Brigade is the
Road to Reform Brigade. We will reform. It is the road.
We challenge you! (*Pledges, clenched fist raised.*)

ROM: I support that. 'No use pining, no use crying, let's
drink and drown it all!'

KHRUNINA: (*Impressed.*) Yes, Andrei. Nothing else.
(*The BAND plays a strong march that has echoes of both the
funeral march and a Red march – and echoing marches of the
German Revolution, and the Spanish Civil War to come, as
well as the Russian Revolution. It starts low. The Brigade
prepares for work, and as they march to it, they sing.*)

COMPANY: (*BAND plays.*) Who doesn't work
doesn't eat.
People who shirk
lead to defeat.

(*Chorus.*)
It's our right,
you know, this fight!

The work we do
is wholly just.
And if it's not
do it we must.
(*Chorus.*)
We can make wealth
without the rich.
Who deals in death
ends in the ditch.

(*Chorus.*)
We see the earth
without commands.
All that has worth
are our demands.
(*Chorus.*)
Those who are free
despise the slaves.
We shall see
whom freedom saves.
(*Chorus.*)
(*The BAND continues playing the march, which rises in crescendo during ZALYGIN's speech.*)

ZALYGIN: (*As if to himself.*) We went to the work-site singing. We sang as we worked. We had to drill by hand, so we ate into the rock rather slowly. We wanted to get the earth out of the pits as quickly as possible. We had wooden cranes. We loaded their buckets with earth. We pushed barrows up and down planks. There was a continuous line of barrows and many banners near them. The noise of the workings reminded me of a huge factory. You can't hear the sounds made by individuals but you can hear all the sounds made by everyone. Piles of mud and rock landing on the earth, horses' hooves clattering at the bottom of the excavation, the blast of explosions, the whistle of electric motors sucking water out of wooden chutes, the sound of axes on wood, the ringing of hammers on steel.

(*ZALYGIN joins the others. VOLKHOV watches from his stool.*)

KHRUNINA: There's rock to blow up.

KREMKOVA: (*Screams.*) I'm a poet.

KHRUNINA: I'll go.

KREMKOVA: No.

(*KHRUNINA goes. The BAND switches to a fast, throbbing tempo.*)

9: 'Faster! Faster!'

The BAND at a fast tempo. The Brigade as in Scene 8. They stand in line but do not move. One or two of them hold picks, two hold barrows, poised to move.

KREMKOVA: Ready.

ZALYGIN: Wait.

KREMKOVA: I'll go.

ZALYGIN: She'll do it.

> (*Over the sound of the BAND, the work-site radio blares. The Brigade is tense and expectant but they gradually become absorbed in Bylov's confession.*)

RADIO: (*A thin, male voice sings.*)
> I had a bunch of fine keys
> and a forger's pen
> but how greatly I envied
> the life of the working men.

RADIO: (*Another voice.*) Faster, comrades, faster! Shame on the shirkers Petrov, Bylov and Sigova. Fyodor Bylov! You are a traitor to the Canal army. Shock workers have their portraits painted. Bylov, we stick up a cartoon of you.

RADIO: (*Bylov's voice.*) Dear Comrade Instructor. For five months, I cut the morning parade every day because I thought even horses die of overwork. No arguments or propaganda did any good. They shamed me at my section meetings. But no-one else knew. But now, a cartoon of me has gone up in the camp, arm-in-arm with a kulak, and written underneath it says, 'You both work together with the class enemy!' I can't go any further. I give you my word: I'll work. You'll see. I'll work and I'll get others to work, so they won't have cartoons drawn of them. I'm ashamed that I wanted to interfere with construction and that I'm a class enemy of the Soviet Government. Signed, Fyodor Bylov. PS: Please take down the cartoon.

> (*The radio goes dead. The BAND stops in mid-line. Silence.*)

VOICES: (*On and off, including the BAND.*) What is it? What's happened?

(The BAND collects round the scene.)
Is Surkov there? Kiskin? Oh Kolya! Sedova? *(A woman.)*
Here I am. Grishin? There he is. So everyone's safe.
Where's Khrunina?
ZALYGIN: Where's Teresa?
(ROM comes from behind.)
ROM: Her face...
(The Brigade parts to reveal KHRUNINA's body lying on the ground. They crowd round. VOLKHOV stands, but stays at his stool.)
VOICE: Who's to blame?
KREMKOVA: It was an accident.
(ZALYGIN takes off his coat and lays it over the body. He turns to VOLKHOV, the Brigade turning with him.)
ZALYGIN: Where were your eyes?
VOICE: *(Shouts.)* Bastard.
ZALYGIN: What sort of work do you call that?
VOLKHOV: She worked, didn't she? You told them to work.
ZALYGIN: Me?
VOLKHOV: She worked like a real man!
KREMKOVA: A real man!
VOLKHOV: You too are real. You seem to he real. You'd attack an old man?
KREMKOVA / ZALYGIN: *(Together.)* Old? A man?
VOLKHOV: *(Like stone.)* It's a task. A matter of honour. They trusted us. The working class has given us a test. The working class – changes the course of rivers. They drain swamps, move rocks. They stand close to dynamite. *(Steps forward, tears the coat off the body.)* Move it. Take it off the bank. Shove it on the edge of the workings.
ZALYGIN: We must bury her.
VOLKHOV: *(Orders.)* Get to work.
(There is no movement.)
ZALYGIN: *(Holds out his hand, looks at the palm.)* It's snowing.
(The light dims over the work site.)

71

10: The Canal Is Completed

May 1933. ZALYGIN moves from the work site into the club room. The others begin to assemble in the room as for a meeting.

ZALYGIN: The first aluminium has been produced at Zaporozhye. At Kuznetsk an open-hearth furnace has been built. The motor works at Gorky has produced its first machines. Stalingrad turns out a hundred tractors a day. Magnitogorsk makes its first pig iron. New cities in former deserts. A new Canal cuts right through the heart of Karelia.
(*Sings.*) And the water
that flowed from the White Sea
was red.

11: 'We Are Changed'

August 1933. The Brigade has all assembled in the club room for a meeting. Their banner 'CONQUERORS OF THE WATERSHED' stands prominently behind them. They address each other as at a conference.

KATZAPCHIK: You ask me to sum up the work. I never thought about it. When I came, not many believed we'd finish. Who believes in miracles? You go for wool and come home shorn. I thought, 'My life's over. There's no way out. Live and then – phut – it's gone.' I don't know if I was right.

ZBYSHKO: When I came I was confused. It really got me. I'm still confused, but it's not so bad now.

KVASNITZKY: It didn't bother me. I beat the drum and went deaf. Still I said to myself, 'I'll keep quiet, and bang my drum when I'm asked to.'

ROM: You're devils, no use to anyone but saints.

ZBYSHKO: Who are saints?

ROM: What saints? I didn't say there were saints.

KREMKOVA: When I came I was confused. Night and day were no different. Noise, lights, noise, work, noise, darkness. When I came I said to myself, 'They won't easily break you!' I organised a shock-work team on Canal section two-eight-two and lock number thirteen.

We declared an emergency to conquer the watershed. It
was the final week of storm attack. We got permission at
two in the morning. At four we started work. It was May
Day. Labour Day. The section was blocked by a fall. We
shifted the boulders and stones. We worked for thirty-
eight hours without a stop. That happened four times.

ORLOV: The White Sea Canal brought me into the family
of workers. Before it, I'd always been alone, following
my own little path. Now I walk the broad road of the
workers. You asked, why did I stay on? Why not take
advantage of the remission granted me? Why, because I
had a little work still unfinished. I volunteered to stay at
the Canal. I engaged in earth-moving operations right to
the end of the project.

KREMKOVA: I learned to admire Comrade Orlov's spirit.
I wrote a poem.
You Russians,
fishers of the universe –
you who scooped heaven with the net of dawn,
blow your trumpets!

Fall on your face,
drop
mug-forward into the swamp.
A new sower
roams the fields,
a radiant newcomer drives toward you,
singing,
his stone mouth
stretched
from east to west.
My husband died at the Canal. I don't know where. It
doesn't matter. I was freed before my sentence expired.
But I stayed. He would have been happy to know that.
To know I've become a fully valued participator in the
socialist construction of our country. Comrade Volkhov
has asked me... I've agreed to sign on for work on the
construction of the Moscow-Volga Canal.

ORLOV: I asked to be transferred there too. But art calls. I
have been recalled to the Aleksandrinsky Theatre,

Leningrad. As an Honoured Artist. I believe we open
with 'The Seagull'. (*Pause.*) There have been many
deaths.

ZALYGIN: Have you got inside the slave, Orlov?
Experienced the sweet delights of the quarryman? From
the inside? When you wielded a pick you were a navvy,
were you? 'Thanks for the experience. Now goodbye.' I
don't even want to speak of you. My report is first of all
about us. We found old, mutilated matter stuffed in us.
Most of it alien. What have we done? I don't live outside
of myself. I contribute to it, give it a form. But I derive
from others. I have no other existence. Work is like that.
It's the product of relations between people. It can't be
made from nothing. We reforged ourselves. Reforged the
dead old twisted matter. And used it again.

VOLKHOV: There's no sense in your preaching, Zalygin.
Now you are free. Face the facts. Look at me. Some
people say, 'He's not been reforged. It's all pretence!'
Well? What if I have been honoured with the Red Banner
of Labour? My work here has been good but I know I
don't deserve that. A thief, a murderer. All the same, isn't
it just? There are so many thieves and murderers, some
little, some big. Even though I was only a little one, if I
can't be corrected, what hope is there for the big ones? If
you ask, 'Why the red banner?' I'd say, 'Look at
yourself.' Perhaps I'm not altogether saved. What of it?
There must be a reason. You too may still be pretending.
There have been deaths. Accidents. For some it was
sacrifice. For the Canal. Was that pretence? Don't ask
me, ask yourselves.

ZALYGIN: She needn't have stood there.

ORLOV: She decided that.

KREMKOVA: It was a bullet.

ORLOV: A stone. The blast.

KREMKOVA: (*To ZALYGIN.*) She loved you.

ZALYGIN: What?

(*ZALYGIN presents VOLKHOV with the Order of the Red
Banner of Labour – a bronze medal hanging from a red ribbon.
He pins it on VOLKHOV's chest. They shake hands. The
Brigade applauds. VOLKHOV presents an award to ROM.*)

VOLKHOV: Accept this, Comrade Rom, on behalf of the
Cultural and Educational Section, in recognition of your
developing musical talent.
(*VOLKHOV gives ROM the wrist-watch stolen from
Khrunina. They shake hands – ROM holds VOLKHOV's
hand in his.*)
ROM: I accept this gift, Comrade Volkhov, not for myself,
but for all the comrades of the Band, now freed, in the
spirit in which it's given – as a mark of the time.
(*They shake hands heartily.*)
May you, one of the exemplary reforged, find health and
happiness in your new post at the People's Commissariat
of Transport. More than that – may you have a long life!
(*They applaud.*)
VOLKHOV (*To ZALYGIN.*) In a day or two, Comrade Stalin
will be sailing down the Canal in the steamer 'Anokhin',
inspecting the work. Frenkel will accompany him. But
it'll be a special day for you – in fact, for us all. Maxim
Gorky will be with him. (*To ZALYGIN, ORLOV and
ROM.*) Do you think you can make something of it? One
last show for the camp leadership? As free men, of
course.

12: Gorky's Pipe

*Aboard the steamer 'Anokhin'. ZALYGIN as Stalin puts on a white
military jacket, summer style. He has a pipe. ROM, as Gorky, puts
on a peasant, smock-style top. He has a pipe. ORLOV, as Frenkel,
puts on the same as in Scene 1, except that the Order of Lenin is
pinned on his leather jacket. He has a cane. They sit in wicker
chairs. They view the environs. They are joking and laughing.*

GORKY: (*Sings.*)
To the sea,
to our blue sea,
to our blue Baltic sea,
sailed a great ship.
(*They laugh. GORKY puffs on his pipe.*)
STALIN: (*Of GORKY's tobacco.*) Virginian?
GORKY: (*Of STALIN's tobacco.*) Georgian?

(They laugh. FRENKEL looks off.)

FRENKEL: This gave us some headaches. The caissons.
Always collapsing. Flooded the workings. There's a lake
over there. It was a pity we had to climb so high. More
locks than I'd have liked. Further down we had to hold
back the River Vyg. Built a dam. Only earth. The spring
floods broke through more than once. Nasty.

(The boat stops. STALIN sits up, alarmed.)

STALIN: What is it?

FRENKEL: Another lock. There's a GPU man.

GORKY: They guard the locks?

(They rise.)

FRENKEL: *(Calls off.)* Comrade!

STALIN: Don't invite him on.

FRENKEL: *(Calls.)* Hello! Here's Comrade Stalin. Yes!
Come to inspect the work.

STALIN: *(Calls.)* Everything…secure?

FRENKEL: He doesn't understand. *(Calls.)* Many ships?

GORKY: A peasant.

FRENKEL: A lot were drafted from the south.

GORKY: Cold for them up here.

FRENKEL: They march up and down.

(They laugh.)

GORKY: *(Calls.)* Where are you from? *(To FRENKEL.)*
Where?

FRENKEL: Kem.

STALIN: Where's that?

FRENKEL: Up there on the White Sea. Transport centre.

STALIN: He knows his Canal.

GORKY: *(Calls, laughing.)* You devils in long overcoats! You
yourselves don't know what you've done.

*(STALIN and FRENKEL laugh modestly. They sit. GORKY
calls again.)*

One thing, comrade. How deep is it just here? *(Pause.)*
What?

(GORKY stops smiling and returns slowly to his chair. Sits.)

STALIN: Karelia breathes! We'll begin work next year
transforming the Canal. Karelia will take a slice of heavy
industry.

GORKY: *(To STALIN.)* I like your portrait. *(Indicates the lock
area.)* A good fifty metres. Wood?

76

FRENKEL: Glazed tiles.

STALIN: You've written a great deal about the nature of
labour, Maxim. You'll find plenty of material for your
enquiries here.
(*The boat moves forward.*)

GORKY: (*Puffs on his pipe.*) Look at that. (*Gestures off.*)
Forest. The wildness of nature. Bitterness. No words
enough. Changes of nature change the world. Changes of
the world change human beings. The 'sensible'
bourgeoisie said it was impossible. Reforging petty
criminals? Little people? Thirty-fivers. Fifty-eighters,
They said it would insult them, reduce them to
humiliation, destroy them. They said we should show
respect. What was our answer? The worker says, 'I don't
fight to kill, I fight to raise the labour of men and
women from toil. I kill only when it's not possible to
eradicate the ancient habit of feeding on human flesh and
blood.' When do people work well?

STALIN: When the plan is well-laid and the cadres are
running it smoothly.

FRENKEL: When they're absorbed in their work. When
they're healthy, new people! And even their clothes are
new!

GORKY: No. When they've entirely eliminated lice.
(*STALIN and FRENKEL laugh.*)

STALIN: The capitalists say in their newspapers we've
killed off a lot of useful people here.

FRENKEL: Lies! What's reforging? It's making people
useful.

STALIN: Several tens of thousands. Perhaps more.

GORKY: The 'diseased' and 'dangerous' people themselves
tell of their cure. All bourgeois are 'masters' but in a
class society everyone is inevitably somebody's servant.
In the old times bandits and merchants sang a song –
In our youth we killed and robbed a-plenty.
In our old age. we must save our souls.
Any capitalist robs more than all the thieves on the
White Sea – Baltic Canal.
(*STALIN rises. To FRENKEL.*)
And you have given Russia the White Sea – Baltic Canal.

(*Gazes at FRENKEL's Order of Lenin.*)

FRENKEL: (*Looks abashed at his Order.*) It's named after Comrade Stalin. The Stalin Canal. It's his gift.

STALIN: A brave act? And a rash one. In war, murderers are heroes and given medals. In peacetime, why shut them up or shoot them? We experience mistakes in our own skin and bones, or the back of the neck. We can't separate theft from the redistribution of wealth, or a murderer from a redeemer. I know about prisons. In my youth I killed and robbed, and I saw what it was like from the inside. As I get older, do you expect me to save my soul? Kirghiz worked here, from the desert steppes. Kalymycks, Tartars. Peasants from Ryazan, the Urals, Altawi and Saratov, Tambov, Chernigov. 'Daddy,' says the little boy, 'what did you dig it with?' 'Picks, my dear. And all America and Europe took off its hat!' 'Daddy. Is it very deep?' 'Rafts of logs float down it, ships with foreign flags, ocean cargo boats and the fleets of our Baltic navy, but nobody can find the bottom. I guess it's half a mile down. And you can't reckon its width, (*Shouts.*) it keeps getting wider.' 'And could a whale swim through it?' 'A whale could swim through it, and a salmon.' 'And could our house swim through it?' 'Our house too.' The little boy says, 'Let me steer the ship.' He blows the whistle and turns the wheel and everyone praises him.

GORKY: Show me a hundred prisoners. After they've done ten years, if five of them emerge as decent men and women, whom should we praise? The measures we employ? Or our Russian courts, which persist in sending so many good, reliable elements?

(*STALIN is looking off. He turns and addresses the audience.*)

STALIN: It has to be rebuilt. It hasn't gone deep enough.

(*FRENKEL sits aghast. GORKY puffs at his pipe.*
VOLKHOV moves up to ZALYGIN.)

VOLKHOV: Comrade Andrei Zalygin. You have made statements undermining the authority of the Soviet Government and damaging the cause of communism. You are under arrest.

(*STALIN takes the pipe out of his mouth. Freeze. Slow fade.*)

A BREAK IN BERLIN

Characters

GERDA

THE WIDOW

PETKA

ANATOLE

The action of the play takes place in a basement room of a bombed-out apartment block in a middle-class district of Berlin over the three days 29 and 30 April and 1 May 1945.

The play is based on an anonymous diary, 'A Woman in Berlin', translated by James Stern, Secker and Warburg, 1955.

Dedication

'There are two problems that are causing Dr Hauptmann great anxiety. To keep the villa warm, so that one can live, we need coal. It has so far been impossible to get any in Waldenburg. Secondly, since Dr Hauptmann has no access to his bank accounts and his royalties are not sent to him, we do not know how we could pay for any coal. In both these matters we ask for your kind understanding and influence.'

Letter from Gerhart Hauptmann's nurse to the General Director of Museums and Protection of Historical Monuments, Warsaw. Dated 5 December 1945, Agnetendorf, Silesia.

One

The ceiling of the room is supported by the trunks of silver birch trees. The walls are cracked. The window has lost its glass and is partly boarded up. A door leading to the rest of the flat is jammed at a crazy angle and unusable. Another inside door leads to a toilet and washroom off. The splintered outside door is unlockable. This door opens on to a slope of packed rubble, which runs up to street level. There is rubble everywhere in the street.

In the room are battered items of once-good furniture – a polished mahogany dining table and two chairs, an armchair with torn upholstery and a blanket lying over one arm, a clothes cupboard of carved wood, a food cupboard, a small glass-fronted china cabinet which is empty and lacks much of its glass, a rather grand but faded sofa whose back has been let down to convert it into a bed with a blanket draped over it. There is a small but rather fine tasselled carpet lying on the floor. In one corner is a sink and a gas stove. Along one wall is an empty, cold fireplace.

There is a large suitcase lying on top of the clothes cupboard. On one wall is a shelf with a few old newspapers, some books with once-fine bindings and a scattering of cheap novels. A small Meissen figure of a modestly dressed woman stands on the shelf.

Enter GERDA coming from the toilet. She goes to the window and leans out. It is spring. The scent of earth. She breathes in deeply. She seems momentarily at ease.

She is thirty, middle-class. She may be blonde, tallish, or dark, medium height. She is restless, vivacious, attractive, mercurial. She is however, very tired. She is wearing a plain but thick, good-quality winter coat over a skirt, slip and blouse. In these clothes she has slept the night, and many nights.

She looks at her watch. She leaves the window. She takes a water glass and goes to the sink. She turns the tap. It is dry. Her pale, tired look returns. She is waiting, waiting.

She sits with her elbows on the table, her chin resting on her hands. There is only a crust of bread on the table. She breaks it and eats it. She goes to the food cupboard, still chewing. The cupboard is bare except for a last tiny piece of butter which, after some deliberation, she spreads on the bread.

As GERDA eats, the WIDOW appears outside in the street. She hobbles along in a pair of down-at-heel but good quality shoes. She stops at the top of the slope to glance briefly at a handwritten notice which has been pinned to a post. What she reads dampens her spirits. She walks slowly into the room.

The WIDOW is forty-ish, a plump dark bourgeoise trying to preserve her never-stunning looks in case times change and her value on the widow market is renewed. This is made less likely by her having across one cheek the scar of a terrible burn. She has dyed her hair for fear the white in it will show. She is dressed in a suit of excellent cloth, though it is dusty with plaster. She has elevated from the petty bourgeoisie and is still capable of considerable vulgarity. She is carrying a bunch of crocuses and a newspaper. She enters the room without ceremony. This is where she lives too.

WIDOW: (*With assumed brightness.*) Aren't they lovely? Found them in the garden next door. (*She puts the crocuses in the water glass.*) Just a little clump. Peeping out of the rubble. (*She is about to put the glass to the tap.*)

GERDA: There's no water.
(*Nevertheless the WIDOW tries the tap – there is no water. The WIDOW puts the glass of crocuses on the table. GERDA gazes at them. The WIDOW dusts herself down. She shakes out the newspaper into its single sheet.*)

WIDOW: Tt! Tt! Look at that! What have they come to?

GERDA: Still no bread?

WIDOW: (*Sits at table.*) No, no bread. Frau Rosen's has had a direct hit. Right through the ovens. (*With satisfaction.*) And right through Frau Rosen. Ach! Curse these shoes. (*Takes off a shoe and rubs her foot.*)

GERDA: (*Looks towards the window.*) It's quieter this morning. (*Sits at table opposite the WIDOW, the crocuses between them. GERDA stares at the crocuses.*)

WIDOW: (*Quietly, almost a whisper.*) Frau Bauer says they're already in Rangsdorf. Apparently they've decided to starve us for eight weeks and when they come they'll take everything we have. In Silesia people are already eating roots. (*She takes the last crust and goes towards the cupboard.*)

GERDA: I finished the butter.

WIDOW: You devil. We said we'd share it. I bet it was sweet.

GERDA: It was rancid.

WIDOW: I told you. We shouldn't have kept it for four weeks. (*She goes back to the table, sits. While she eats the crust she reads loudly from the newspaper, her eyes growing round.*) 'Sixty-four-year-old chemist's wife ravished.' 'Nun violated twenty-four times.' Did she count them? Telling them on her rosary? (*Adopts the attitude of a nun at devotions.*) Eighteen – nineteen – twenty... What's the matter, dear? (*She has swallowed the last crust of bread.*)

GERDA: (*As she gazes at the flowers.*) Nothing.

(*The WIDOW forgets the newspaper and she too stares silently at the flowers for some time. It is as if the crocuses mesmerise them.*)

WIDOW: (*Breaks the silence.*) Aren't they beautiful?

(*GERDA takes a crocus out of the glass and eats it. The WIDOW watches her completely devour it. She puts her hand on GERDA's.*)

(*Quietly.*) Keep your coupons safe. I heard there'll be potatoes at the corner tomorrow.

(*The rumble of guns begins. They look up at the ceiling.*)

GERDA: (*To herself.*) When will they get here? (*She stands. She goes to the window.*)

WIDOW: (*Reads from paper.*) 'Reinforcements are marching to Berlin from south and north. Salvation is nigh. Victory is certain.' (*Confidentially.*) 'That man' knows exactly what he's doing, believe me.

GERDA: (*Returns to seat at table, guardedly.*) Yes. Yes, you're right. We can rely on him.

WIDOW: As upon the Lord.

(*GERDA puts her hand to her head.*)

A pain, is it dear?

GERDA: My period started this morning

WIDOW: Well, I must say! This is a nice time to choose. No water and no bread. And them...virtually in your front room.

GERDA: It's always on time.

WIDOW: Why did you have no son, Gerda? No son to make a soldier? After all the calls to give us children. A widow lives at peace if she has the son of the soldier she loved.

GERDA: I don't know if I'm a widow.

WIDOW: (*Incredulously.*) You have pure, healthy blood. He was racially good. There was a battle for babies.

GERDA: Please.

WIDOW: You let your career stand in the way. That's what it was. As for me, I stayed at home with the Führer. It was there I fought the battle for the existence of the race. I had three soldiers and two girls. 'Give us children and guns.' I gave up my job to devote myself to propagation. With your husband a lawyer you could do no less. The Führer himself couldn't have asked more of me. But you, Gerda, your career defaced your national value. It came between you and your duty to preserve the blood.

GERDA: (*Bursts out.*) Please stop! (*Distractedly.*) Don't you think you should be more careful!

(*The roar of heavy guns. GERDA looks up at the ceiling.*)

WIDOW: And look. Look at this! (*Holds up the single news-sheet.*) This is all you can bring out!

GERDA: They released me at the newspaper until further notice. (*Rises, goes to window and looks out.*)

WIDOW: And why, I wonder?

GERDA: They hadn't enough newsprint.

WIDOW: They hadn't enough labour enthusiasm.

GERDA: Huh! Even the typists were sent to the printing works. Twelve hours a day. But not to do printing. To assemble prams, they were told. But they discovered it wasn't prams at all. It was tanks. More tanks.

WIDOW: And you not being a typist. In fact, as your husband's...

GERDA: There were no stories coming in. Nothing for me to do.

(*The hissing, whizzing and howling of a shell, followed by an explosion. Masonry falls somewhere. They jump up, looking at the ceiling.*)

WIDOW: Of course, the likelihood is the trees will stand up even if the house collapses.

(*The WIDOW stands on a chair and pulls down the suitcase from on top of the cupboard. She begins to pile her personal belongings into it. It already contains a good deal. She adds her sewing box, medicine box, clothes from the clothes cupboard, including a yellow silk blouse, the Meissen figure from the shelf, some books.*)

GERDA: The landlord's parting gift before fleeing to the Amis – half-a-dozen birch trees cut down in the Tiergarten. (*Pause.*) There was a woman yesterday in the bread queue. Her sister said they were already Russian.

WIDOW: Already Russian?

GERDA: Tanks rolling in, the Ivans laughing.

WIDOW: Why didn't you tell me?

GERDA: Our women went out into the street, she said. Waved. Held up their children.

WIDOW: Who said?

GERDA: The woman.

WIDOW: Did they? Where was that?

GERDA: In Mullerstrasse, in Wedding.

WIDOW: Wedding! Yes, they might do that in Wedding! But not our women. You wait. I've spoken to refugees. There was a young girl when I went for potatoes, she'd walked all the way out of Prussia. Just sixteen. They'd had her. Front and back. A dozen of them. She looked sixty.

GERDA: She's still going for potatoes.

WIDOW: (*Loudly.*) We haven't spent four good years and lost the flower of our manhood fighting the Bolsheviks only to parade our children for them when they come. We're Germans, not animals in a zoo.

GERDA: (*Looks around instinctively.*) Don't you think...

WIDOW We've stood all sorts of sacrifices but that isn't one I'll stand.

GERDA No, of course not.

WIDOW I've always said I'll never cower before them.

GERDA: That was all very well then. But now...

WIDOW: Well?

GERDA: (*Laughs it off.*) It's going to be different, isn't it?

WIDOW: Gerda! You're not saying it's the end, are you?

GERDA: I never said anything of the sort.

WIDOW: This is only a setback! My dear, you haven't read the notice they put up last night. It commands every man to fight in the defence of the city. Now whatever did I do with that tie-pin?

GERDA: Another notice? (*She goes to the door.*)

WIDOW: (*Loudly after her.*) You have a look! It's signed by Hitler and Goebbels.

(*GERDA stands at the door, looks out to left and right, goes to the notice pinned outside. She reads it in an expressionless voice. The WIDOW searches for the tie-pin.*)

GERDA: (*Reads.*) 'Summons to the Population of Berlin. Fight to the last drop of blood! There will be no surrender! Surrender will be punished by death by hanging or shooting. Warning! Private Hans Koch threw down his rifle in Braunauer Street. This traitor is hanging by his neck at the railway station as a lesson to all. Fight for the Führer, for the final victory of the German nation. Until victory!' Hand-written! Huh! It only shows how low they've sunk! (*As if to herself as she enters.*) When will they get here? (*Goes to the sink and takes a bucket.*) I'll see if there's any water at the pump. (*As she crosses the room to go the WIDOW takes her by the arm and detains her a moment.*)

WIDOW: (*In a loud whisper.*) I've tied my wedding ring to the elastic of my panties. If they get that far I shan't mind any more about the ring. (*Laughs.*)

GERDA: (*Laughs as she goes.*) You don't want a ring. You want Siegfried's sword.

(*Goes. The laugh vanishes from the WIDOW's face.*)

WIDOW: She always slandered our great Wagner. It's a wonder to me they never took her away. After all I said. Perhaps it slipped down the side. (*Searches for the tie-pin down the side of the armchair seat.*) Her husband was too high up, I suppose. Gruppenführer Ratenauer. That's a title! No! (*I.e. 'No tie-pin here.' Resumes her search.*) Well, it wasn't for want of trying. I know they were grateful. Otherwise I couldn't have kept my flat. A fallen hero for a husband, but the widow is turned out of her rooms because of the housing shortage? No, they were grateful. A lot of what I told them was true, after all. (*Nods.*) Yes, they were grateful, they were. Pity the flat was bombed. (*Looks in the grate.*)

GERDA: (*Enters with the bucket of water.*) What are you looking for?

WIDOW: My husband's tie-pin.

GERDA: Not again.

WIDOW: It has such lovely filigree work. Well! (*Slams the case shut, stands on the chair, heaves the case back on top of the cupboard.*) What's it like?

GERDA: Hardly a soul. That shell hit the cinema. The whole front's caved in. The poster for 'Baptism of Fire' is flapping in the wind, all charred, bits of it are tangled round a lamp-post. (*Laughs.*)

WIDOW: (*Holds her face in her hands.*) Uh! I could do with a nice warm wash.
(*The WIDOW fetches a saucepan and GERDA pours water into it. GERDA places the bucket at the sink. The WIDOW takes a match, switches on a tap at the stove, strikes the match. There is no gas. The match goes out. She sniffs the gas ring.*)

GERDA: Oh no! (*She sits on the sofa.*)

WIDOW: Never mind! A cold wash braces you up.
(*The WIDOW pours the water from the saucepan into a bowl in the sink. There is no soap. She washes her face, arms and hands and dries herself on a none-too-clean towel. As she washes.*)

GERDA: Couple of lumps of coal on the pavement outside the chemist's.

WIDOW: Well, run and get it then. There's plenty of wood around. We might find more coal...

GERDA: (*Of the grate.*) Huh! In that! It would smoke us out.

WIDOW: Build one in the street.

GERDA: Too much wind. You do it. I'm tired (*Curls up on the sofa, pulls up the collar of her coat.*) It's still so cold. You wouldn't think it was spring.

WIDOW: (*Drying herself.*) Yes, a cold wash drives away sleep. (*Takes off shoes to wash her feet.*)

GERDA: Oh God. (*Gets up gingerly.*) Give me the water. (*The WIDOW goes for the bucket.*)

No, in the bowl. I'll use the same. Quickly.

(*She takes the bowl from the WIDOW and goes into the toilet, off. The sound of her washing. The WIDOW, barefoot, waits.*)

(*From the toilet.*) Uh! It's cold.

WIDOW: I'm glad I'm rid of that, anyway.

GERDA: I met Frau Lehmann at the pump. Her milk's dried up. With little Hans six weeks.

WIDOW: What did you say?

GERDA What could I say? Wait till the warm weather?

WIDOW: Chew a piece of bread and when it's nice and soft stick it in his mouth.

GERDA: Yeh?

WIDOW: Yes, it's an old trick the peasants use, so my nurse told me. Of course, that was some time ago. She used it herself. In the Great War.

GERDA: Hand me the towel. (*The WIDOW passes the towel behind the toilet door.*) Who'd give her the bread? (*Pause.*) She'll have to wait for the Ivans.

(*The roar of heavy guns. The WIDOW looks at the ceiling. GERDA emerges from the toilet, straightening her skirt and coat.*)

WIDOW: She what?

(*GERDA puts down the towel and goes back to the toilet. The sound of her pouring away the dirty water.*)

GERDA: I bet they make sure they're eating.

WIDOW: But you know, Gerda, they won't give any to us.

GERDA: No, they won't.

WIDOW: They'll take everything we have.

GERDA: Yes. That's right.

(*The sound of GERDA trying, but failing, to flush the toilet.*)

WIDOW: (*Irritably.*) There's no point in doing that. Where do you think it's going to go?

(*GERDA emerges.*)

GERDA: I've no idea.

(*The WIDOW takes the bowl, pours some water into it and bathes her feet. GERDA returns to the sofa and curls up on it, pulling up the coat collar. She is restless. She gets up. She goes to the shelf and takes a battered old novel. She returns to the sofa, curls up as before. Opens the book. Reads silently.*)

WIDOW: Or there's wild herbs and plants. Nettles are good. So are dandelions.

GERDA: It isn't the season.

WIDOW: More's the pity. (*Pause.*) I found some dandelion leaves yesterday. I didn't tell you. I was on the way to the bank.

GERDA: With your pockets stuffed with 'little portraits'. They're valueless, you know that.

WIDOW: No, they're not. They guaranteed that. The bank was still there. There was actually somebody working in it. I paid the money in. It's all right, Gerda.

GERDA: (*Stops reading.*) That was a major decision!

WIDOW: You didn't know I had a thousand marks stuffed in this chair, did you? Well, I did. A thousand marks, and nothing to buy. They guaranteed it. Look. (*Unfolds a slip of paper she has taken from the pocket of her suit.*)

GERDA: Tomorrow, the bank... (*Makes the sound of an exploding bomb.*)

WIDOW: But I'll have this! (*Waves the paper. She folds it and puts it away carefully in her pocket.*)

GERDA: You should tie it to the elastic of your panties. (*Reads book. Silence. The WIDOW dries her feet.*) Frau Lehmann's heard another rumour. Ribbentrop and von Papen have flown to Washington. It seems the Amis and the Tommies have fallen out with the Ivans. They want to ally themselves with us to keep Ivan out.

WIDOW: (*Looks around, startled.*) Gerda, are you crazy? Do you know what you're saying? Of course you're cynical. The nation demands greater faith than anything you can offer. (*Puts shoes on.*) It relies on its stalwarts, men and women of my perseverance. (*Stands.*) We have marched all over Europe with that tenacity. I will not relinquish it in my nation's hour of greatest need. (*Pours water away.*)

GERDA: All right, you know all about that. (*The roar of heavy guns. They look at the ceiling. Pause.*) (*Reads in upper-class accent.*) 'Helmut threw a glance at the untouched meal, got up from the table and pursued Katarina into the garden. "Katarina," he shouted, "the bierwurst!"'

(*GERDA throws the book down. She sits up, feet on the floor. She buries her face in her hands. The WIDOW sits in the armchair. She holds a handmirror. She adjusts her pinned-up hair.*)

WIDOW: You must be praying, Gerda.

GERDA: You must be joking.

WIDOW: 'Need teaches prayer.'

GERDA: Like hunger teaches begging.

WIDOW: You shouldn't speak disrespectfully. You never know when you'll need Him.

GERDA: (*Scoffs.*) I don't need the Lord when I have the Führer.

WIDOW: Gerda, remember what I said, or someone will teach you a lesson. (*Puts mirror down, pulls blanket around herself.*)

GERDA: All those wonderful lessons!

WIDOW: Oh, if only you had a man to keep a rein on you.

GERDA: I've got one, haven't I? The greatest son of the nation! Huh! What do I want a man for? The glorious strong men totter, and with them the myth 'man'. Pathetic, weak and helpless men! They have no male privilege now they've lost the privilege of killing. Back from the front they come, wounded, feeble, defeated. The war is a man's business. If 'we' lose it, it's not us who're defeated, not us Germans. It's German men.

WIDOW: Oh, so we're not going to be defeated after all? I'm glad you have that opinion. We're going on, then – men or no men? Though I wouldn't put it quite like that.

GERDA: Oh, how daring! It just means blood! blood!

WIDOW: Well, look at you! That's nature too.

GERDA: That's my own, not someone else's.

WIDOW: They sacrifice their own.

GERDA: And other people's.

WIDOW: That's their own, their sacrifice. Gerda, don't think I don't know what you mean. (*Puts her hand to her face.*) Look. There's the mark of my life. I've never talked about it. Why should I talk of our shame? A phosphorous bomb burnt our block to a cinder. I lost my face. I lost my sons. Not on the battlefield. In their beds! Only one of my children escaped, my daughter. My

oldest son I found in the rafters of the house next door –
hung there by the blast, stuck like a pig, dripping his fat,
barbecued. One day, it was raining, I sang 'The Song of
God's Counsel' and buried him in the garden. His coffin
was a broom cupboard. So, don't think I don't know. But
for me it's finally some kind of glory. A holiness,
although terrible. My husband knew that, we both knew
it. If you're talking about strength, the strength to go on,
that is my strength. He had it too.

GERDA: Yes. A lawyer-turned-soldier would have.

WIDOW: Don't be cynical about others. It'll only turn back
on you.

GERDA: Don't be cynical! Isn't that what you're being?
Massively, absolutely cynical?

WIDOW: I believe in what's splendid.

GERDA: You're mad.

WIDOW: And you are level-headed.

GERDA: Yes. I'm being realistic.

WIDOW: How terrible!

GERDA: Terrible! Well then, that's splendid!

*(GERDA jumps up in exasperation and goes to the door. She
looks out. The WIDOW gets up, takes the newspaper and
pulling another old paper off the shelf deliberately opens
them out in the grate. She sets light to them. They burn with
a flickering, brief intensity, the smoke drifting into the room
from the blocked chimney. At the doorway GERDA is counting
to herself in Russian.)*

WIDOW: What are you saying?

GERDA: Nothing.

*(She counts. She goes out, tears down the notice in the street,
returns to the room screwing it up.)*

WIDOW: It doesn't sound like German.

GERDA: It's just numbers.

WIDOW: Numbers?

(GERDA throws the notice into the fire.)
What's that?

GERDA: The notice. *(Counts.)* It's Russian.

WIDOW: *(Shocked, in a whisper.)* May God preserve you.

(*GERDA lies down on the sofa in her winter coat, pulls the blanket over her. The WIDOW sits in the armchair, takes off her shoes, rubs her feet.*)

GERDA: What is it? Corns?

WIDOW: My feet swell when I get excited.

GERDA: Let's hope it stays quiet.

WIDOW: Yes. (*Pause. Of the shoes.*) These were a really good pair. Gerda.

GERDA: Yes?

WIDOW: Despite all you've said, you know, you're still a German.

(*Silence. No answer. The WIDOW sinks further into her chair. GERDA is counting to herself.*
The lights dim to a blackout.
The roar of bombers approaching. A massive air-raid develops. Bombs explode far and near. Bursts of flame as they explode – a blinding light in otherwise total darkness.
The red glow of burning fires shows the extent of damage to the saturated city. The absolute silence of dawn spreads.)

Two

A far-too-silent eerie silence. It is twilight. A soldier appears. He goes down the slope into the house. He stands just inside the door. He is armed. He carries a flashlight with which he sweeps the room. He picks out the faces of first the WIDOW, then GERDA, then back briefly to the WIDOW, then back to GERDA to study her closely.

He goes into the room, looks through the door and into the toilet. He tries the jammed door. He rummages for weapons in cupboards and drawers, knocking over the crocuses, a chair, the table. To this soldier the room is like Aladdin's cave.

As he approaches them, the two women get up and retreat to a corner, taking their blankets with them, while he searches the sofa and the armchair.

Day is dawning. The soldier switches off his flashlight.

The soldier is PETKA, a peasant. He is short, broad-backed with a round head, cropped, blond hair and yellow, jaundiced skin. He is well-fed, unperturbed and smells of alcohol. He spits regularly and copiously on to the floor, usually to emphasise a point. He takes special pleasure in spitting on this floor.

A radiant dawn breaks. The sky is blue, the spring sun shines brilliantly. PETKA looks around. GERDA invites him to sit. PETKA shakes his head.

GERDA: (*Softly.*) Can I help you?
    (*PETKA starts, shakes his head.*)
PETKA: You speak Russian.
GERDA: A little.
PETKA: Any weapons?
GERDA: No. No weapons.
PETKA: I speak German. (*Tries it.*) Schnapps! (*Laughs.*)
GERDA: (*Laughs.*) Yes. Schnapps!
PETKA: Well?
GERDA: No. No Schnapps. (*Pause.*) No food. (*Pause.*) Have you any food?
PETKA: Yes, yes, plenty of food. (*Looks around, glances at the WIDOW.*) Is this your house?
GERDA: No.
PETKA: Whose is it?
GERDA: I have a room here. I did have. Upstairs. This lady – she had a house. In Ringstrasse. She was bombed out, too.
PETKA: Where's the landlord?
GERDA: (*Laughs caustically.*) Oh! he escaped.
PETKA: (*Gestures fleeing.*) Ran away! (*Laughs.*)
GERDA: (*Laughs.*) That's right.
WIDOW: What is he saying?
GERDA: He's asking about Herr Golz.
    (*The WIDOW nods.*)
PETKA: What's that? (*Indicates the WIDOW's scar.*)
GERDA: It's a disease.
PETKA: Uh! A disease?
GERDA: A skin disease.
PETKA: Och! Bad skin! Bad blood.
GERDA: Yes.
WIDOW: What is he saying?

GERDA: I told him you have eczema.

(*The WIDOW nods.*)

PETKA: (*Looks around room.*) I congratulate you on your repairs. The master woodcutter recognises an expert when he sees one.

GERDA: It stands up.

PETKA: (*Gazes at GERDA.*) Have you a husband?

GERDA: Yes.

PETKA: Where is he?

GERDA: I don't know. Not far.

PETKA: What's your name?

GERDA: Gerda. What's yours?

PETKA: Petka. Petka the Woodcutter.

(*Laughs. So does GERDA. Suddenly.*)

Do you know what love is?

GERDA: What?

PETKA: Love.

GERDA: Oh.

PETKA: Have you heard of it?

GERDA: I've heard of it.

PETKA: Do you know what it is?

GERDA: You mean true love?

PETKA: (*Laughs.*) Yes. True love.

GERDA: Yes, I do.

PETKA: Ah! (*Nods.*) Passionate love. You know about that?

GERDA: Yes, yes, passionate love. Do you love me?

PETKA: (*Startled.*) What?

GERDA: Do you love me?

PETKA: Yes. Yes, I love you. I have wristwatches. (*Points to two watches strapped to his wrist.*) You love me.

GERDA: You are very nice. (*Retreats a step.*)

PETKA: Yes. Nice. (*Follows her.*)

GERDA: (*Stares into his jaundiced eyes.*) You are not well.

PETKA: (*Doesn't understand.*) What?

GERDA: You're not healthy.

PETKA: I'm quite healthy. (*Advances.*)

GERDA: You're a soldier. You must be busy. (*Retreats.*)

PETKA: The war is over.

GERDA: Not yet. (*Reaches the outside door and slips out. As she goes.*) You're a bad one. (*Laughs.*)

(*GERDA runs up to the street where she waits. He follows her immediately. He sizes up the situation.*)

PETKA: I'll be back. (*Goes.*)

(*The WIDOW stands the furniture upright. GERDA goes in, she retrieves the crocuses. The WIDOW freezes. They both stand in the middle of the room as if mesmerised.*)

WIDOW: What shall we do?

GERDA: There's nothing we can do.

(*They wait.*)

WIDOW: Can't we go somewhere and hide?

GERDA: This is where we went. This is where we're hiding.

(*They wait.*)

Will he come back?

WIDOW: I think so. What did he look like?

GERDA You saw.

(*They wait.*)

WIDOW: Did he say what his rank was?

GERDA: (*Angrily.*) Why worry about his rank? (*They wait.*)

WIDOW: So long as there's only one. (*Goes towards the grate, where there is a heavy iron poker.*)

GERDA: Don't be crazy. (*The WIDOW stops. They wait.*)

(*Enter two figures – PETKA, bringing with him ANATOLE. First Lieutenant ANATOLE is a heavily-built Party man from the Ukraine. In civilian life he is a worker in the dairy of a collective farm. His father was a worker, his mother a peasant.*

He wears a jacket and belt and over it a leather overcoat with stars on the shoulders. He carries a cap with a star and he wears high leather boots. He wears on his chest the Stalingrad medal, a modest decoration composed of a thick copper medal on a multi-coloured ribbon wrapped in cellophane. He is armed with a pistol in a holster.

He keeps himself well groomed. He is well-fed and generally his manner inspires a feeling of reliability and confidence. He reads books but by GERDA's standards he is unsophisticated, a child of the people. He is well informed on the war, on Party history and debate, and on the Ukrainian resistance to the Nazis. He is on a level with the lower ranks socially, drinks and chats with them as equals. When he harangues them on May Day he urges his men, with a look in his eye, to 'make merry' but 'bear in mind the Ukas of Comrade Stalin'. With them, as with PETKA, he is friendly, trusting, almost childish. With a woman of the middle class like GERDA, he is unsure of himself though he does not think he shows it much. He prefaces much of what he says with a brief all-realising, sharp 'Ah!' while raising his head. It is as if he were saying, 'That's how it is! – it's to be expected!' – a mixture of surprise and imperturbability. He does not speak about his Stalingrad exploits, whatever they may have been. He accepts his own wilfulness, his pertinacity in war, with the determined ambivalence with which he bears his own weakness – his sense of fatality.)

PETKA: That's her.

ANATOLE: (*Inspects the tree trunks, sings.*)

'And then the hunters,

Deep in the forest...'

(*Walks all the way round GERDA.*)

Is this what Goebbels sicked up?

GERDA: It's nice to hear good German spoken.

ANATOLE: Ah! A classy bitch, just as he said. Quite the lady. Come on.

GERDA: Not with me.

ANATOLE: (*Mimics.*) 'Not with me!' (*Seizes GERDA by the throat.*) Didn't you know 'ladies' are coming down a step or two now?

(*ANATOLE pushes GERDA on to the sofa. The WIDOW screams and hides in a corner. GERDA scrambles off the sofa and puts a table between herself and ANATOLE. ANATOLE edges round the table towards her. PETKA laughs. ANATOLE grabs GERDA by the throat and pushes her violently across the room towards the toilet. GERDA screams.*

The excited PETKA joins ANATOLE and together they push GERDA who falls backwards through the door into the toilet. ANATOLE backs off, leaving PETKA with GERDA, who is crying.)

(*Bowing out of the toilet.*) After you! (*Turns to the WIDOW.*) In our army, dear Frau, we share everything. (*Laughs.*) Don't be frightened. You're all right. Even the peasants are well off with us. Look at Petka. He has the best of that bargain. I expect you find it outrageous. Excuse my German. It's a little sore.

WIDOW: Rusty.

ANATOLE: Ah! She speaks. Yes. A little rusty. I learnt it at the Party school. My teacher was a German from the Volga region. You notice the difference.

WIDOW: Yes. It's a savage kind of German.

ANATOLE: Savage? It's country speech, I suppose.

WIDOW: It won't be understood in Berlin.

ANATOLE: No, not by your type. (*Pause.*) What do you think of us?

WIDOW: What?

ANATOLE: What did they say? Your leaders? After all, we were expected. They must have told you something.

WIDOW: No.

ANATOLE: Surely…about this?

(*Gestures towards the toilet. The WIDOW doesn't answer.*)

These things, you realise…they musn't happen.

WIDOW: Musn't happen?

ANATOLE: No. They're forbidden. By order of Stalin.
(*Shrugs.*)

(*The toilet door opens. PETKA emerges, grinning.*)

PETKA: Go on then. (*Laughs disgustingly.*)

(*ANATOLE takes off his overcoat, goes to the door.*)

ANATOLE: (*To GERDA.*) My apologies. But if Comrade Petka has finished, would you care to join us in the dining room? (*Gives a mocking bow, turns away into the room.*) Petka, these ladies would like something to eat and drink. See if there's anything to spare in the field kitchen.

(*PETKA is still sniggering.*)

Petka! The smoked sturgeon! This instant!

PETKA: (*Mocks an affected accent.*) At once, Tsar Anatoli.
(*Goes.*)

ANATOLE: (*To WIDOW.*) You see? Petka will bring you something to eat.

WIDOW: That is very good of you.

ANATOLE: Ah! Yes, I agree. You might not have thought we would do such things. Have you a husband?

WIDOW: Yes.

ANATOLE: Where is he? (*No answer.*) At the front?

WIDOW: He was killed. In the bombing.

ANATOLE: Ah! (*Nods.*) What was his job?

WIDOW: He was a lawyer.

ANATOLE: An officer?

WIDOW: No. Yes.

ANATOLE: In the army? (*No answer.*) The SS? (*No answer. The WIDOW looks away.*)

(*GERDA enters from the toilet, battered, dishevelled, still trying to straighten her clothes. ANATOLE bows to her mockingly.*)

Now the 'lady!' (*To WIDOW.*) No offence to you, dear Frau. (*To GERDA.*) Our peasants have a very clear orientation, once they've made up their minds. I will see he doesn't bother you again. As a matter of fact, our Petka is really quite a kindly soul. You will see. He has gone to get some food for you, and something to drink. Don't be frightened. It won't have done you any harm. Our men are all healthy. Petka's as fit as a bull. A little jaundice in one eye. But nothing wrong lower down, so he tells me. And I believe him. He may not be gentle. So what? You are not his sister. (*Laughs.*) Shall we be sentimental? A little crudely so? Berliners like that, I believe. Do you know any Russian songs? No? Well, you'll see. Petka will bring some vodka. We can drink to The End of the War, to Victory. What do you say? Of course, it's our victory, but you can't drink to defeat, can you?

WIDOW: Why don't you go?

ANATOLE: But I've only just come, dear Frau. We've fought rather too far, and seen rather too much, to be able to leave so early. No, I must point out we will be here for some time. (*Seats himself on the sofa.*) Well, well, this is smart. Just feel the upholstered.

WIDOW: Upholstery.

ANATOLE: Upholstery. Thank you, dear Frau. (*To GERDA.*) You see, my lady, she's helping me out. She's quite a good friend. She already told me about herself. She must be a good friend to you too. Is she? I'm sure she is. Look at her. A plump, money-grubbing, careerist, bourgeois bitch. Aren't I correct? She has had too much for too long and still isn't satisfied. Of course I'm correct. (*To GERDA.*) There's something different about you. You have a brain in your head. A writer? A doctor? An engineer?

(*GERDA scoffs.*)

Well, something of the sort. Definitely a woman worth having...with us. Tell me what you do. There's a lot I could ask you to do. Eh? Have you a husband?

GERDA: Yes.

ANATOLE: Ah! She can speak. Where is he?

GERDA: I don't know.

ANATOLE: At the front? (*Silence.*) If it's the eastern front, he's likely to have had a cold grave.

GERDA: I don't know where he is.

ANATOLE: What's his name? (*Silence.*) Comrade Petka says your name is Gerda. (*Silence.*) You will have to hand in your identity papers. I like Gerda, such a nice name. (*Suddenly.*) Did you ever have anything to do with the Party?

GERDA: (*Quickly.*) No, never.

(*Pause. ANATOLE scrutinises her. Laughs.*)

ANATOLE: I meant the Communist Party. (*Silence.*) Not likely! If you had, you'd have forgotten all about it by now, wouldn't you? Just a regrettable mistake. A youthful aberration. All that's behind you. Yes, it's a closed chapter, over and done with. You have had to say it so often, it's been checked and double-checked. But now, of course, all that's changed. Changed again. It's an open book once more. Eh? (*To the WIDOW.*) Don't you agree?

(*The WIDOW has grown wide-eyed at the drift of ANATOLE's speech.*)

WIDOW: Yes, of course.

ANATOLE: (*To GERDA.*) And you? (*Bitterly.*) Gerda Ratenauer.

GERDA: (*Quickly.*) How did you know my name?

ANATOLE: Perhaps you had a careless friend?

WIDOW: (*Blabs.*) I didn't...

ANATOLE: You? Who said anything about you? And that's not a skin disease either. (*To GERDA.*) My dear Gerda, you don't think we'd take all this trouble to come to Berlin without a list of the best addresses? (*Laughs.*) We were right. You were here. Ready. Waiting. I must thank you for your warm reception. (*Sees PETKA returning.*) I and my comrade will be only too pleased to accept your gracious offer, but we will take our lodging here only if we may bring our board with us. You see?

(*PETKA enters with several grubby bottles of vodka, some black bread, some lengths of Polish sausage and something greasy done up in newspaper. He has been drinking. He goes straight up to GERDA with the sausage.*)

PETKA: The minutes without you have been endless. I have returned just as soon as I could. Believe me, Gerda… (*Hesitates.*) No, I don't like Gerda. Natalya. You remind me of Natalya. (*Reflects.*) Yes, she will have left school now. I'll call you Natasha. Please. (*Holds out the sausage and leads GERDA to the table with it.*)

ANATOLE: Petka, you are disgusting.

(*GERDA sits down at the table.*)

PETKA: Well, Anatoli? Hasn't your Petka tamed the German bitch?

(*PETKA puts the sausage on the table and cuts slices of it. He gives the knife to GERDA who cuts more sausage and takes some bread to go with it. She eats ravenously, using her hands. The WIDOW is tempted to the table. She brings some plates and knives and forks. She places the food on the plates. PETKA unwraps the newspaper. Like a conjurer, he takes two salt herrings out of the greasy packet and holds them up delightedly.*)

From *Pravda* – the bitter truth!

(*He stuffs one herring into his mouth and throws the other on the table. The WIDOW hastens to put it on a plate, where she cuts it up. Part she gives to GERDA, part she keeps. She eats with a knife and fork. ANATOLE surveys the happy scene.*)

Tuck in, Anatoli. Don't miss the best of the flesh. Not again. (*Guffaws.*)

ANATOLE: (*Smiles, with heavy sarcasm.*) I would never have thought it possible! Russians and Germans sitting down together! Sharing hearth and home!

PETKA: Aren't you hungry? (*Pulls the herring bones from his mouth, piles them on the table. Beams at GERDA and the WIDOW.*) You see. We bring you a treat. (*Opens a bottle of vodka. Pours some into glasses.*) We've come all the way from Stalingrad just to have dinner with you. You'll see we're kind. As kind as you could want. Come on, let's drink, ladies. Natasha! To Friendship!

(*He raises his glass to GERDA's, drinks the glass dry. GERDA drinks very little. PETKA refills his glass.*)

Here we are, dear Frau! To Friendship! (*Doesn't wait for a reaction from the WIDOW, drinks.*)

WIDOW: What is he saying?

GERDA: He's drinking to Friendship.

WIDOW: He should put his meat on his plate.

(*PETKA sweeps the herring bones on to the floor. Ignoring the plate, he uses the table as he presses slices of sausage on to his bread with his thumb.*)

PETKA: Friendship is the noblest thing in the world. Or anyway between the Volga and the Elbe. What is war? War is war. I haven't grown fat on it, but I like it. It's like an elder brother, nice and reliable, and always there. Peace! Don't give me peace! Peace is a prick-tease. Yes she will, no she won't. War ends, it seems you're going to enter bliss at last, you grow perfectly rigid with hope, then – who would have guessed – clunk, down comes the sabre and your dicky-dock goes split-splat on the good black earth once more. No, you can depend on war. There's no 'all men are equal', or 'human brotherhood' or any of that shit. You can only really be friends in war, or anyway at the end of a war – war settles it one way or another who is making friends with whom. (*Drinks. As if introducing himself.*) Petka! Petka Furmanov! From Molotov. Not the person, the place. Don't all stare. On a fine evening the girls call me the spirit of Siberia. It's May Day tomorrow. (*Sings.*) 'I'm going to fly to my lover by the river-bank at midnight. We will dance till I sweat spunk. She will be my only one. The spirit of summer,

for the night.' (*Drinks.*) You don't know our May Days.
Och, they were not like that under the Tsar. Peasants like
me? We couldn't have chopped off heads in the meadows
under the moon with impunity. With impunity! What a
word! Our leaders make sure we go to school nowadays.
I couldn't speak as I've spoken here under the Tsar, may
the devil take him. Even now there are places where you
can't find 'with impunity'. There is nothing like it in
Molotov. I haven't even heard it in Lisovije Sorochintsy.
But in Kiev. Now, in Kiev I hear it every day. It makes
you think, doesn't it? You understand, ladies, the strength
of the Soviet system. How else could I be so happy?
(*PETKA sings his version of a Ukrainian resistance song,
'The Song of the Partisans'. As he gets wilder, GERDA and
the startled WIDOW take cover.*)
Daylight waned, the stars shed light,
On we journeyed through the night.
On a village house we lighted,
But we inside were not invited.
Just as soon as we had halted
All the doors were firmly bolted.
Still we stayed, as we were bold,
And shouted loud, 'It's very cold.
So, good women, don't be frightened,
Don't let partisans be slighted.
Let us in. You'll be delighted!'
Am I right, eh comrade? Am I right!
ANATOLE: Yes, Petka. Absolutely!
(*ANATOLE joins in loudly. He takes a few dance steps, stamps
hard in his leather boots. As they sing, PETKA goes on the
rampage round the room, more and more drunk.*)
PETKA / ANATOLE:
At last there came what we were seeking,
Her front door she set a-creaking,
And with sausage all were treated,
And with vodka we were greeted.
So we spent the night together –
Partisans, peasants in one tether.
Nothing didn't we try our luck in

Till we'd had our fill of...

(*PETKA, swigging vodka, has been smashing things, sweeping objects on to the floor, knocking over the table and a chair. He seizes the suitcase from on top of the cupboard, opens it and showers the contents on to the floor. He loses his place in the song, repeats lines haphazardly. He sweeps crazily on until finally he falls flat in a drunken stupor in a corner. After the case has scattered its contents, the others are silent. ANATOLE's song trails away. Amongst the contents of the case on the floor is a Nazi flag. They stand about it, staring at it, variously amazed, perplexed and frightened.*)

ANATOLE: What is this?

(*The WIDOW looks guilty.*)

WIDOW: A flag.

ANATOLE: I can see it's a flag. What kind of flag is it?

WIDOW: The German flag.

ANATOLE: No, it's not the German flag.

WIDOW: (*Frightened.*) It's the Nazi flag.

ANATOLE: Yes, the Nazi flag. The flag of barbarism and destruction. The flag we have torn down and wiped in the dirt in every town and village between here and Moscow. (*To the WIDOW.*) Why have you got a Nazi flag?

GERDA: Everyone had to have one.

ANATOLE: Maybe, but everyone hasn't kept it. What does it mean to you now? Eh? Tell me?

WIDOW: It means there'll be a Reich for a thousand years.

GERDA: She's just stupid.

ANATOLE: (*Walks over the flag, twists his boot on it.*) There's your thousand-year Reich, you bitch.

WIDOW Have you a flag?

ANATOLE: What? (*With sarcasm.*) We have the Red Flag, didn't you know?

WIDOW: I can make one for you.

ANATOLE: What?

WIDOW: I have a steady hand. I sew very neat hems. Look. (*Holds up the hem of the flag.*) I can take out the middle, you see.

ANATOLE: Eh?

WIDOW: It's the same red. I have my sewing box. I have some scissors. I'll make you a nice red flag.

ANATOLE: Ah! The dear Frau is most anxious to help us.
She is already thinking about the May Day celebrations!
A truly willing German! Can we even turn her into a
comrade? That would be a miracle. And we don't believe
in miracles. Go ahead. And make the hammer heavy and
the sickle – make it sharp.

(*ANATOLE kicks the flag to the WIDOW who scrambles to
collect it all up. She runs about the room rescuing her scattered
belongings. She stows them away in the case, only putting
aside scissors, pins, needle and thread, and the yellow silk
blouse. She returns the suitcase to the top of the cupboard.
Finally she sits in the armchair and starts work, sheepishly,
guiltily, fearfully.*

*GERDA sets the furniture to rights. ANATOLE bends over
PETKA, shrugs, goes and sits at the table.*

*Through the following speeches, the frightened WIDOW works
silently at the flag. She cuts the stitches of the black and
white swastika design and removes that part of the flag. She
cuts the shapes of hammer and sickle out of the yellow silk
blouse and sews them in the top left-hand corner. She is
oblivious of and, of course, does not comprehend the talk
between ANATOLE and GERDA. She finally nods off, falling
fast asleep in her chair.*

ANATOLE attempts to strike up a conversation with GERDA.)
The front has reached the Landwehr Canal.

GERDA: Has it? (*Sings a sentimental song.*)
'There lies a corpse
in the Landwehr Canal!'

ANATOLE: What's that?

GERDA: A song. What did it sound like?

ANATOLE: There'll be more than one corpse there now.
(*Produces a map of Berlin from a cellophane folder in his
pocket, opens it out on the table.*) A hundred and thirty of
your generals have surrendered. I didn't know you had
so many.

GERDA: Whose generals?

ANATOLE: (*Points out the position of the front on the map.*)
There is the Canal.
(*GERDA is close to him as they look at the map.*)
This is the district. Where are we exactly? Ah! This is
the street.

GERDA: No. This one.

ANATOLE: Malmbergstrasse. Yes.

   (*GERDA's hand is pressed on the table as she leans over the map. ANATOLE puts his hand on hers. She moves away.*)

GERDA: What's your rank?

ANATOLE: (*Laughs.*) My rank? First Lieutenant.

GERDA: (*Reflects.*) Oh! And your name?

ANATOLE: My name is Anatoli.

GERDA: Anatole.

ANATOLE: (*Laughs.*) Shouldn't you ask my name and then my rank?

GERDA: Not in Germany.

ANATOLE: Ah!

   (*Laughs. Then GERDA laughs.*)

   Well. Let me ask – What is your husband's rank?

GERDA: (*Vaguely.*) Oh, he's an officer.

ANATOLE: Was he taken prisoner at Stalingrad?

GERDA: I told you I don't know where he is.

ANATOLE: But you do know his name. And yours is not Ratenauer. You are not married.

   (*GERDA is startled. Pause.*)

   Come, Gerda. I've taken you into my confidence.

   (*Indicates map.*) See if you can be a little more...bending. You can see we haven't cut ourselves off from you. The German Party has always kept its good people in mind. And not only those with such excellent Russian. It'll be necessary to find Franz. If you can't, we will. Of course, it must seem a long time ago.

GERDA: Yes, a very long time.

ANATOLE: Don't you really know where he is?

GERDA: No, I don't. I've had no letter...

ANATOLE: You and Franz worked closely together, didn't you?

GERDA: If the war hadn't broken out we would even have got married.

ANATOLE: But you never did.

GERDA: No. When he was called up, that dream was over. He wouldn't hear of it. 'What? Bring more orphans into the world?' he said. He was one himself, from the Great

War. (*Hesitates.*) Well, that's how it was. He went off to
the east. I stayed in Berlin, in the flat. There was the
bombing. Bam! The place went up. In spite of that, we
feel as united as any married couple. Except that…
I haven't heard from him for a year. (*Pause.*) His last
letter came from the Ukraine. (*Pause.*) I can hardly
remember what he looks like. All my photos were
destroyed in the bombing. I had one picture of him, I
carried it in my handbag. But when the news got worse, I
destroyed it – he was in uniform. He is only a corporal,
but I was afraid. (*Looks at the WIDOW at work at the flag.*)
I'm not sure if I should speak like this.

ANATOLE: Go on.

GERDA: She denounced me. She lived in the same block.
She got hold of a file from her husband's office. It had
details of various investigations. She found my name on
it, as she thought. Gerda Ratenauer, wife of
Obersturmführer Ratenauer. I always made out I was
married. She must have reckoned she'd landed a really
big catch. She told her husband what she knew of me.
They thanked her and promoted her husband. They
arrested the Obersturmführer and came for me. But I was
able to say my 'husband' was away at the front. They
realised their mistake. They let the other Ratenauer go.
Then they started to look for Franz. They took me in for
questioning – rather more than straight questions and
answers. But I didn't tell them anything. Eventually they
let me go. They'd heard Corporal Franz was…a very
good soldier, and they doubted her word. They came to
the conclusion she was a jealous old bitch. 'All this we
owe to the Führer!'

ANATOLE: The Führer? Yes, you're right. But you can't
blame Hitler personally. Capitalism produces Hitlers
and amasses the materials for war. In my view, the
German and Russian economy complement each other.
A Germany built on socialist principles could become
Russia's natural partner.
(*GERDA warms to him against her will. For a moment she
believes he is treating her as an equal partner in conversation.*)

GERDA: When you say that, something of the old life comes back, from when German men were clean and could speak. Now they're dirtier even than us women. Do you know what they said, even before you came? 'Go on and be raped, for God's sake, or you'll get us all into trouble.' That's the measure of their vileness. Cowardly, useless. (*Directly at ANATOLE.*) A man would not approve of such things. He sees in a woman a comrade. Doesn't he? I am a German, but I speak your language. I saw your birch trees. I was in Moscow when I was young. (*Laughs.*) On a painting holiday.

ANATOLE: I'm from the Ukraine.

GERDA: I saw the villages in your Ukraine, I sketched peasants in straw sandals, the tumble-down cottages you are so proud of. (*Changes tack.*) Oh yes, our women are so much flesh. Conquer us and it's like adding paprika to meat. Perfumed, manicured, coiffured meat. There is really nothing like us in your villages. You lay out the meat straight on the table. We use plates, Anatole. Knives and forks. At least you have shiny leather boots nowadays, and a clean uniform, a red star on your cap and ribbons on your chest.

ANATOLE: Yes, things are changing. Germany had no need to go to war. After all, it was a rich, cultivated country. It was only necessary to fascism. Industry was highly developed in your cities. It needed raw materials, markets. So it started a war for them. In your villages, phew! Every peasant has a drawer crammed full of linen. Even a wardrobe. Our peasants, you know, can store everything they have in one room. A few hooks on the wall to hang all the clothes. And the dirt! When you Germans take a broom you sweep the filth out of the house. With us, we push it under the cupboard. On the back of the living room door is a towel – you would think it was for drying your face and hands. No, it's where all five children blow their nose. Did you see those posters in the Moscow trams? 'Wash your face and hands every day, your body once in ten days, your hair every month.' Washing – and shining your boots. With us, that is 'Culture'!

GERDA: Culture, yes!

ANATOLE: We had the revolution and began to build industry. Your war wrecked all that. But we have fought the invaders and conquered. Russia stands on the threshhold of a great development. Look at this wood. (*Runs his hand over the table.*) Finely polished. Look at the carving on that cupboard. The carpet you should have rolled up and put away – it is too good to allow our coarse Russian boots to stamp all over. You Germans planned to conquer with polished steel. But underneath the polish, (*Bangs the table.*) you were rotten. Your steel was not enough. Inevitably, you were defeated. The sick conqueror comes home, himself conquered. (*Suddenly.*) You know, I'm in charge of the milk in my collective farm.

GERDA: (*Laughs.*) The milk?

ANATOLE: Yes. It's a huge dairy. More than a thousand cows.

GERDA: What are you? Foreman?

(*ANATOLE nods.*)

It's a responsibility.

ANATOLE: Huh! It isn't so hot. Milk, milk! (*Laughs.*) Nothing but milk.

GERDA: (*Laughs.*) Just what I thought. What a great bear you are!

ANATOLE: What?

GERDA: A bear. (*Uncertainly.*) You know, a bear.

ANATOLE: A bear is an animal. It is brown. It lives in the forest. It's very big. It growls. I am not a bear.

GERDA: (*Laughs.*) I made a mistake.

ANATOLE: Yes, you made a mistake. Why are you laughing?

(*GERDA stops laughing. Pause.*)

GERDA: (*Bursts out.*) Then why did you let him?

ANATOLE: Who?

GERDA: (*Screams.*) Him!

ANATOLE: Oh Petka. That was Petka. They are animals.

GERDA: You grabbed me by the throat. Is that comradely?

ANATOLE: Comradely? Who said anything about comradeship? Don't be mistaken. You are still a German.

(*GERDA is crushed. Pause.*)

GERDA: A man would not approve of it.

ANATOLE: What man? Where is he? Tell me where I can find such a man. (*Pause.*) Not even a man in charge of the milk. (*Pause.*) Give us a thousand years.

GERDA: (*Cries out, despairingly.*) A thousand years?

ANATOLE: You're behaving like a schoolgirl. (*Leaves her.*)

GERDA: You have made me loathe my own skin. I can't touch it. I can hardly bear to look at it. Huh! My mother told me I was one of those pink-and-white babies. The pride of a mother's heart! The last thing my father said to her before he went off to the Great War was, 'Whatever happens, don't take her into the sun without her lace bonnet.' I didn't only have a lace bonnet. I had a white crocheted shawl. And when they bathed me, they tested the water with a thermometer.

ANATOLE: Ah! You were rich.

GERDA: No, not rich. I had the usual bourgeois comforts. (*As it strikes her.*) There's a lot you don't know.

ANATOLE: Yes. Have you heard of Pushkin? Of course you have. Once Pushkin was travelling through the Ukraine. He saw the poverty, the stupidity, the disease, and he wrote, 'They should not be so buried, for they are alive!' We had another poet, the great poet of our national liberation struggle, Taras Shevchenko. He wrote about life in the countryside. He was persecuted, told to stop writing. So he wrote,
'Oh bury me, but rise you up
And break your heavy chains
And water with the tyrants' blood
The freedom you have gained.'
You see? Blood for blood. I don't know much. What do you know about fascism?

GERDA: Fascism?

ANATOLE: Yes, fascism. Would you please explain the meaning of the word.

GERDA: Well, fascism...it comes from Italy. Mussolini. The Latin, 'fascio'. Meaning a bundle of rods.

ANATOLE: Rods? The type that beat? Yes. Corpses in dust.
Corpses in mud, corpses in water, corpses in snow.
Ukrainian villages in flames. Old women turning over
bodies in village graves. That's not in the dictionary.
(*Produces a shabby cardboard wallet from his pocket and takes
a photograph from it, puts it in front of GERDA.*) Look.
That's her.

GERDA: Your wife?

ANATOLE: You've guessed. Do you think she looks old?

GERDA: She must be older than you.

ANATOLE: No, the same. German women are so slender.
(*Brightly.*) What would you be like if I took you back
home – to my mother – she'd feed you up. Yes, on fat
chickens! And cream. (*Of the photo.*) You'd be just like
her. Before the war we lived well enough. But you're
educated. You've travelled, you've seen my country.

GERDA: It's a beautiful country.

ANATOLE: Yes, fine, proud Ukraine! The Nazis tore
through us and ripped us apart. They stopped short of
Kiev and plundered the countryside. Then they rolled
on, leaving behind gangs of collaborators – businessmen,
old landowners, nationalists, fascists – slavery and
slaughter. In my country education is esteemed.
Knowledge pays well. We need it. If you were Russian
you could get a highly paid job in Kiev, Chernigov,
Kharkov.

GERDA: Thank you very much. When you have some
leave you can take me there. I'll bring my sketchpad and
paint the corpses.

ANATOLE: 'Leave.' What is 'leave'?

GERDA: Holidays from the army.

ANATOLE: Ah! Holidays! I have been fighting since 1941.
Four years. (*Takes another old brown photo from his wallet.
Looks at it.*) My son. (*Hands GERDA the photo.*) He was
two then. Now he'll be six. I've no idea where he is, or
his mother. They could be anywhere in the Ukraine.

GERDA: You must find them. (*Looking at the photo, laughs.*)
He's so ugly! His hair is just bristles.

ANATOLE: I'll find him. There'll be time for that.
(*GERDA returns the photo.*)

GERDA: (*Bitterly.*) Four years. It explains a lot.

ANATOLE: Maybe his head has been smashed against a wall. Did you know the brains of children are sometimes not so pink? Yes, I can imagine you in your lace bonnet, sitting in your white crocheted shawl in the straw in the corner.

GERDA: Not in the straw!

ANATOLE: No? Well, I can imagine the bonnet and shawl. You must have been pretty. You are still pretty. One of our women your age is nothing more than a milk cow. I tell you, I like you. You're a woman and not a baby-factory. You've got hips and two breasts, but I look at your face first. You are thinking, independent. You look capable. In our country you would be an engineer, like my sister.

GERDA: An engineer with a neck.

ANATOLE: A neck? Yes, I like your neck. Why?

GERDA: So you do. You like to put your hands round it.

ANATOLE: That was when I'd looked at your hips.

GERD: Oh. And when you look at my face, you kneel and pray.

ANATOLE: No, I feel happy, equal, safe. I needn't be lower than you or higher than you. I can stand alongside you and look at the world.

GERDA: I have no evidence of that.

ANATOLE: You have plenty of evidence. I show you the map of Berlin. I empty my wallet. Now look! (*Pulls everything out of his pockets.*) A man loves a woman when he allows her to see what's in his pockets.
(*His pockets reveal his identity card, all manner of papers, a savings bank book. They are worn, faded, grubby.*)

GERDA: You have allowed me! (*Of the photo on his identity card.*) Here is the man revealed. Is it really you? You must have been twenty when they took this, still wet behind the ears. Now he allows a woman to look at it. Well! He has certainly grown up into a splendid First Lieutenant.

ANATOLE: (*Tosses a faded photo in front of GERDA.*) My sister.
(*GERDA looks at the photo.*)

They raped her to death.

(*GERDA gazes at the photo. She looks round the room. PETKA is asleep, breathing heavily. She sees the WIDOW is sleeping. She stares at the flag. GERDA takes off her skirt under her overcoat and sits on the bed/sofa with her legs under her. ANATOLE takes off his jacket and sits beside her.*)

GERDA: I have a period.

ANATOLE: A what?

GERDA: I have my time. The time of the month.

ANATOLE: Ah! I'll leave you alone. Just let me lie by you.
(*Lies full-length, knees raised. He is very tired.*)

GERDA: If you want to you can touch me. (*Lies beside him.*) You'll have to be careful. You don't mind, do you? (*No answer.*) Wait. I stuffed myself with cotton.
(*GERDA goes into the toilet.*
ANATOLE stretches out his arms to either side, stretches out his legs.
GERDA returns. She stops as she approaches the sofa, seeing his boots.)
You can't wear those.

ANATOLE: What? (*He is tired.*)
(*GERDA kneels, pulls at one of ANATOLE's boots. It won't budge.*)
Leave it alone.

GERDA: Do you sleep with them on?

ANATOLE: (*With weary emphasis.*) They are soldered on.
(*GERDA laughs, shrugs, sits on the bed. She shies off, gets up, looks at the WIDOW, looks at PETKA, goes to the window, looks out. She goes to the table, sits, pulls her coat and the blanket from the armchair around her.*)

GERDA: I'll sleep here.
(*Very quickly ANATOLE gets up, pulls her to the sofa and pushes her down. GERDA does not cry out. ANATOLE lies by her. He does not touch her. Silence. PETKA still lies unconscious. The WIDOW sleeps, the flag over her lap, the needle in her hand. The lights dim. Darkness.*)

Three

The next morning. May Day. Silence, except for the howl of a few distant shells. ANATOLE and GERDA lie asleep. ANATOLE still has on his shirt and boots, GERDA her blouse. GERDA's coat and the blanket roughly cover them. ANATOLE's jacket lies on the floor. His boots stick out over the end of the sofa.

The WIDOW stirs. She rubs her feet. She puts her shoes on. She gets up, the flag drops on to the floor in front of her. She rubs her eyes.

WIDOW: (*Closely, intimately, half-awake.*) Good morning, my Führer! (*Looks around. Sees flag, recovers quickly.*) Ach! It is not possible! My heart can never forgive. (*Puts her needle and thread away and folds the flag. She tidies herself up. Sees PETKA. Recollects. Feels inside her skirt for her ring.*) No. At least, not that. Not that, at least. (*Begins to tidy up the mess.*) Look at it! Oh it's disgusting. Where did they go to school? Of course, they have no schools. I do not understand them. They are people with no sense at all. However do they manage themselves? (*Wipes spittle off the table.*) What can their homes be like? Spittle. Cigarette ends. Their mothers are to blame. (*Sees the filthy carpet.*) German mothers would never permit it. (*PETKA stirs. The WIDOW quickly picks up the carpet, shakes it at the door, rolls it up and, standing on a chair, pushes it away behind the suitcase on top of the cupboard. PETKA slowly rises. The WIDOW finds the Meissen figure of a woman lying on the floor. Its nose and both arms have been broken off.*)
Ayah! She has done no better. The arms must be here somewhere.
(*She searches for the arms on the floor. PETKA is up. He clears his throat, spits on the floor in front of the WIDOW, seemingly obliviously.*)
WIDOW: (*Screams.*) You short-arsed barbarian bastard! This is my floor you're spitting on.
(*PETKA grins. GERDA wakes. ANATOLE turns over.*)
ANATOLE: What is it? (*Goes back to sleep.*)

WIDOW: Gerda, tell this laughing hyena to keep his spittle for his fatherland. It's so green it would pollute his own piss.

(*PETKA frowns, does some morning exercises.*)

PETKA: Well, dear Frau? Got out of bed the wrong side?

GERDA: She's a bit feverish, I expect. It's the late nights.

(*GERDA swings her legs over to sit on the edge of the sofa. She plays with the medal on ANATOLE's jacket.*)

PETKA: I'll fetch her a cold compress. (*Takes bucket.*)

GERDA: (*Sleepily, puts her hand on ANATOLE's back.*) Anatole.

PETKA: (*To WIDOW.*) A moment, dear Frau. (*Goes to door with bucket. Turns back. To GERDA, seriously.*) Take care. I understand some words. 'Piss.' 'Fatherland.' She does not speak ladylike. Petka's telling her. (*Holds up a finger. Goes.*)

WIDOW: What's he on about?

GERDA: Watch out. (*To ANATOLE.*) Are you awake, Anatole?

(*Again the howl of distant shells, GERDA looks towards the window, ANATOLE turns over on to his back.*)

ANATOLE: What is it? (*Sighs.*) What's the problem? (*Of the howls.*) The battlecocks are crowing.

GERDA: There's no problem. Are you getting up?

ANATOLE: (*Sits up, stretches, notes the carpet has been moved, smiles, raises a boot, cries out.*) Ah! I've got cramp.

(*ANATOLE gets off the sofa, pulls up his trousers, walks up and down to ease the pain in his toes. He sees the folded flag.*) Is it done?

WIDOW: Yes,

ANATOLE: Give it here.

(*Unfolds the flag. The hammer is somewhat small and the sickle is twisted. GERDA laughs.*)

You've made it badly. With those, how could you hammer the iron or harvest the rye? Or even smash a Nazi skull. (*Throws it back at her so that it drapes her, covering her head and face.*)

WIDOW: (*Uncovers herself.*) Is it all right? It cost me my best silk blouse.

ANATOLE: For the red flag, only the best...! Hang it up.
(*The WIDOW wonders where.*)
At the window.
(*Grudgingly the WIDOW drapes the flag at the window. The hammer and sickle may be seen from inside and out. ANATOLE paces the room, exercising his toes inside the boot. GERDA stretches painfully. She still plays with the medal.*)
GERDA: What did you get this for?
ANATOLE: For Stalingrad. (*Sings in a low voice as he paces.*)
Don't let partisans be slighted.
Let us in. You'll be delighted!
(*The WIDOW finds one of the Meissen arms on the floor.*)
What's this, dear Frau? (*Takes the figure, holds it up.*)
She is beautiful. But her arms.
WIDOW: Your worker hero.
ANATOLE: What a shame.
WIDOW: He wanted to show his friendship, you remember. No friend of art.
ANATOLE: To Petka, dear Frau, this is not art. It is pornography.
WIDOW: I'll put it away.
(*The WIDOW takes the pieces, wraps them in paper and laboriously climbs to the suitcase, lifts the lid and places the package carefully inside. Takes a hand mirror from the case. Another howl of distant shells.*)
ANATOLE: They must be holding out somewhere. (*Looks at his watch.*) Gone seven. (*Winds the watch, goes to the window.*) Where's Petka? (*Sings in a low voice as he dresses.*)
At last there came what we were seeking,
Her front door she set a-creaking.
(*To GERDA.*) Even your worst sofas are a cut above our best beds.
GERDA: Stop singing that.
WIDOW: That is a very good sofa. (*She is about to perform her morning toilet.*)
GERDA: It's nice to sit on, too.
WIDOW: My husband bought it in Paris. (*Lets her hair down.*)

GERDA: I don't think he bought it. (*Contradicts.*) Anyway, it isn't yours. It's Herr Golz's. God knows where he got it. New York, I expect.

ANATOLE: Ah! I have experienced a very pleasant introduction to the capitalist system.

GERDA: I'm glad you liked it.

WIDOW: (*Screams.*) My comb! He's stolen my comb!

ANATOLE: I hope I may get to know it even better.

WIDOW: The soldier-boy! He's a thief!

ANATOLE: But it is very strange. You don't know where the sofa came from?

WIDOW: He's not content with desecration. He has to steal.

ANATOLE: Dear Frau, be sensible. What could Petka want with a comb?

WIDOW: It is the property of the German nation.

GERDA: Use your nails.

WIDOW: There is no limit to their abomination.

(*GERDA gets up stiffly. She is in her slip. She is sore. She takes her skirt. She crosses painfully to the door of the toilet. She pauses, glancing inside. From the street come sounds of voices over a loudspeaker making an announcement in Russian. GERDA and ANATOLE listen to it while the WIDOW struggles with her hair. GERDA looks questioningly at ANATOLE.*)

ANATOLE: It's May Day. (*Pause.*) It says there'll be meetings.

(*Following the announcement an accordion starts playing the Internationale. GERDA goes to the window. She leans on the windowsill and looks out.*)

GERDA: May Day! (*She peers with difficulty up at the sky.*) Such a blue sky! Do you think a rat feels like this when it looks out of its hole? (*Turns from the window, surveys the room.*)

ANATOLE: It's for you as well as for us. (*He is dressed. He combs his hair.*)

GERDA: This filth? Yes, I know.

ANATOLE: No. The Internationale.

(*The WIDOW has done her best to fix her hair in pins and is putting on fairly heavy make-up. GERDA leaves the window just as the Internationale comes to an end. It is followed by an expectant silence. ANATOLE is adjusting his Stalingrad medal. The sound of Stalin's voice comes over the loudspeaker. It is a little louder than the Internationale. Stalin is giving his May Day greetings to the Russian soldiers, Russian workers, peasants and intellectuals, and to the international working class. He praises the Russian army for its victories and commends the workers and peasants for their efforts in production backing up the war effort. Immediately Stalin begins, ANATOLE stays still, listening intently, looking straight ahead. GERDA puts on her skirt, then also stands still, listening, looking at the floor. Only the WIDOW moves, obliviously putting on her make-up.*

In the middle of Stalin's speech PETKA enters. He carries a bucket of water and under the other arm is a pillow-case full of sugar (about 5lbs of it). He clutches in his hand some candles, a tin of milk and some cigars, and from his forearm on a string dangles a slab of salted bacon. In his pocket he has a Russian army newspaper. He has already had some vodka.)

WIDOW: (*Accusingly.*) Where did he get all that?

PETKA: Liberated some best bacon.

(*He puts down the bucket (it spills). He slams the bacon on the table. The WIDOW jumps. She has a look inside the pillow-case.*)

GERDA: What is it?

WIDOW: Sugar! White sugar!

PETKA: (*To WIDOW.*) The broom, dear Frau.

WIDOW: What?

PETKA: Get me the broom. (*Makes brooming movements. Slops water over the floor, using his hand as a cup.*)

WIDOW: What are you doing? (*To GERDA.*) What did he say?

GERDA: He wants the broom.

WIDOW: Whatever next.

(*She fetches the broom from the toilet. Stalin's speech has ended.*)

PETKA: (*To GERDA.*) Did you get that? (*Sweeps the floor.*) Thanks to the determined efforts of millions of soldiers, workers and peasants the Soviet Army has occupied Berlin, Nazism is defeated, and the Allied powers are victorious. Stalin's May Day greetings to the workers of the world. Strong stuff, eh?

GERDA: Yes.

WIDOW: (*Of the sweeping.*) Tell him not to bother.

GERDA: It's doing no harm.

PETKA: (*To ANATOLE.*) Are you giving a speech today?

ANATOLE: (*Smiles.*) Yes, I'll relay Comrade Stalin's message.

PETKA: Good. I like your speeches. They're matier than most.

ANATOLE: I'm glad you think so.

PETKA: Above all, they're short.

GERDA: I thought he made quite long speeches.

PETKA: That is to a lady, dear lady.

WIDOW: (*To PETKA.*) Did you steal my comb?

PETKA: What? (*Stops sweeping.*)

WIDOW: (*Gestures combing of hair.*) My comb, you imbecile.

PETKA: Has she got fleas?

GERDA: She says you stole her comb.

PETKA: (*Assumes fury.*) Steal? Me? Petka the Woodcutter, steal? I'd rather go to Siberia in winter than steal a thing from her. How could Petka steal anything from a lady? It's not his custom. It's not often he gets to meet a lady. There's nothing like it in Molotov. (*Goes on his knees before WIDOW.*) Believe me. Petka would rather steal wood from a woodyard than touch a hair of a rich woman.

(*Takes WIDOW's hand, makes as if to kiss it, the WIDOW jumps back.*)

WIDOW: You're all wet.

PETKA: (*Gets up, spits.*) She doesn't understand devotion. (*Finishes sweeping.*)

(*GERDA has tidied up the sofa. She and the WIDOW convert the 'bed' back into a sofa. PETKA watches them in amazement. Puzzled, he examines this magical piece of furniture. ANATOLE cuts himself a slice of bacon. He takes the army newspaper which sticks out of PETKA's pocket, opens it out. PETKA stands amazed.*)

GERDA: (*Having watched him.*) There's nothing like that in Molotov!

PETKA: Och, Natasha, I bow before this icon of friendship. (*Bows to the sofa.*)

WIDOW: Does he like the sofa? (*Goes right up to PETKA with the plate in her hand on which she has placed a slice of bacon she cut.*) You like the sofa? Good German sofa! (*In an access of enthusiasm, actually gives the plate of bacon to PETKA. Cackling hugely, to GERDA.*) He certainly likes our sofa, doesn't he, Gerda?

(*PETKA takes the bacon in his hands, puts down the plate.*)

GERDA: Huh! (*Laughs.*)

PETKA: (*To GERDA.*) What's all that?

GERDA: She's pleased you appreciate our hospitality.

PETKA: (*Chews, moved.*) What did I say? Everywhere you go, there is Friendship! (*Clears his throat with pleasure, spits.*)

WIDOW: (*Furiously.*) Stop that! And put your bacon on your plate.

(*She does it for him. PETKA is utterly uncomprehending.*)

PETKA: (*Shrugs, to GERDA.*) The lady has a bad mood this morning.

GERDA: A little nervous. It's her class background.

PETKA: (*Fully understands.*) Is that it? (*To the WIDOW.*) Please accept my apologies. (*Bows, eats bacon.*) If I do anything against your customs, (*Spits out some rind.*) dear lady, I beg you to take into account I am a peasant who cuts wood in his spare time and doesn't know the ways of rich ladies like yourself.

(*The WIDOW looks surprised, looks at GERDA.*)

GERDA: He says he's sorry.

WIDOW: I should think so too. (*Prides herself on her little bourgeois victory.*) Perhaps they'll learn after all.

(*Opens the tin of milk. PETKA lights himself a cigar, throws the match on the floor.*)

Gradually.

ANATOLE: (*Reading.*) Most of Berlin is ours.

PETKA: (*Puffs.*) You know, they've made fires in the street. They're burning stacks of books, newspapers. There was a fat German tearing pictures out of a book. I had a look. 'What are all these big fat books?' I said. 'Nazi literature,' he said, and shoved some more pages into the flames.

'Well then,' I said, 'you don't only want to burn the pictures.' I took the books and chucked them in. They didn't burn very well but they didn't half sizzle. They were cooking meat over the flames. A horse stopped a shell on the corner.

(*The WIDOW drinks some milk, screws up her face. It is sour. She hastily adds some sugar, which she spoons from the pillow-case.*)

ANATOLE: (*Looks up from paper.*) Today, in Russia, it is a holiday. Even here the troops will be celebrating. They will be issued with a special ration of vodka.

GERDA: Oh dear.

ANATOLE: It is also a reward for their war enthusiasm. I suppose your heart isn't in it. I understand. It's hard to accept. What does it matter, though? One cock's as good as another.

GERDA: There's a profound Russian saying.

ANATOLE: Ah! It's international. But you're right. We are no Casanovas. We have to work ourselves up with vodka or else we remember our manners. 'My sweet Anyushka,' 'My darling Natasha,' and blushes and sheepish grins – and we can do nothing. Drink drowns all that, it permits us to get to the point. Even then there's no guarantee of success. Vodka is an unreliable ally of the prick. For you, of course, none of that matters. (*Looks at his watch.*)

GERDA: (*With heavy sarcasm.*) Not in the least.

ANATOLE: (*Folds paper, puts it in his pocket.*) My dear Gerda. It is time for me to go.

GERDA: (*Looks at PETKA, looks at her watch. To ANATOLE.*) Do you have to? It's only half-past-six.

ANATOLE: Yes, there are meetings today. (*Looks at his watch.*)

GERDA: Oh yes.

ANATOLE: It's half-past-seven. You're an hour out.

GERDA: (*Takes off her watch, shakes it.*) Half-past-seven?

ANATOLE: Yes. (*With emphasis.*) Moscow time. Expect me late this afternoon. You permit?

GERDA: (*Caustically.*) Oh yes, I permit. (*Adjusts her watch.*)

ANATOLE: Good. (*Solemnly kisses GERDA on both cheeks. Warmly.*) Until then! (*To WIDOW, formally with a slight bow.*) Dear Frau! (*Commands.*) Comrade Petka!

PETKA: Coming, Comrade Anatoli. (*Takes a swig of the WIDOW's milk. They go. GERDA goes to the window.*)

WIDOW: Whatever next!

GERDA: (*At the window.*) 'Be back from the office at seven as usual, darling.' (*Goes to table.*) Huh! The red bourgeoisie stakes its claim! (*Cuts herself some bacon.*)

WIDOW: Even drank from the same glass. Never in my life have I been so offended. (*Recollects. In a loud whisper, hurriedly.*) Gerda, he didn't... (*Indicates toilet.*) Did he?

GERDA: (*Laughs.*) No, he was flat out. You escaped by the length of a bottle of vodka. (*Feels pain.*)

WIDOW: Ah! Thank God. (*Sees her pain.*) My dear! (*Understands. The WIDOW immediately climbs on to a chair to reach the suitcase.*) The German nation is knocked over and dragged through the mire. (*She drags the case down.*) It is outrageous. Odious. (*She gets off the chair, heaves the case, dumps it, opens it.*) I never thought I would live to see the day.

GERDA: (*Chews meat.*) Well, you have lived.

WIDOW: I could not have faced my husband after what's happened.

GERDA: You talk as if it had happened to you. (*The WIDOW has found the medicine box. She takes out a jar of vaseline.*) I don't think I can eat any more of this.

WIDOW: Here. This'll help.

GERDA: Well! Thank you. You're a knowing old bitch.

WIDOW: That's unkind. I never so much as looked at another man. (*The WIDOW slams the case shut and returns it laboriously to the top of the cupboard. GERDA goes into the toilet with the vaseline.*) Aren't you afraid of him?

GERDA: (*From within.*) Petka? No, I have Anatole as a shield.

WIDOW: I mean him. Anatole.

GERDA: Oh that. No. There's my period.

WIDOW: That won't last for ever, my dear.

GERDA: Somehow I feel I'll be lucky. What's the old saying? – 'A much-used path grows no grass.' I just feel I can seal myself off from anything growing.

WIDOW: I should get yourself something.

GERDA: Huh! I tried. The chemist had condoms. Scattered all over the floor in bits of glass. But nothing for women. They were always short of them. Not an item that was high on the list of priorities of our beloved Führer. (*Comes back in.*) You said yourself only yesterday. The imperative need for German children! In a twinkling (*Snaps her fingers.*) – not a contraceptive in the shops. (*The WIDOW has again assumed her role of mistress of the bourgeois home. Using a cloth, washing soda and some water left in the bucket, she has been rubbing down the mahogany table to try to erase the rings of alcohol. She pauses.*)

WIDOW: Perhaps I put it in my medicine box by mistake. (*Drops the cloth. Climbs up for the suitcase.*)

GERDA: God! You're not still worrying about that tie-pin? (*Takes up the cloth, rubs.*)

WIDOW: Don't be like that, Gerda. It's gold. (*Takes down the suitcase, finds the medicine box.*)

GERDA: Much good it'll do your husband. Not even gold will raise him now.

WIDOW: No, it's not there. (*Finds a broken comb. Closes the box, returns it to the case, closes case, returns it to the top of the cupboard.*) I wonder what I could have done with it. It could have flown into a corner yesterday in that... (*From her vantage point she scans some possible hiding places.*) He never wore it, actually. He always complained it pricked his chest. (*Pulls the carpet from behind the suitcase.*) And I gave it to him on our fifth wedding anniversary! (*Gets down, carrying the carpet. Lands heavily.*) Oh my feet! (*She carries the carpet to the door. She looks left and right along the street. As surreptitiously as possible, she shakes the carpet. She brings it in and lays it on the floor.*) Gerda! (*Presses the broken comb into GERDA's hand.*) Would you mind? I must see to my feet.

GERDA: (*Left holding the comb.*) Well! As you rightly put it – whatever next?

(*The WIDOW pours the remaining water from the bucket
into a bowl, shakes into it some bicarbonate of soda which she
finds by the sink and, taking off her shoes, sits down on the
armchair and bathes her feet. On hands and knees GERDA
combs the tassels of the carpet.*)

WIDOW: Brrh! (*The water is cold.*) That's better. Well? What
do you think of them?

GERDA: What, them? They're men.

WIDOW: I haven't met any like that before.

GERDA: I don't suppose you have.

WIDOW: I suppose your Anatole is more like a gentleman.
But he's still very rude. (*GERDA winces with pain. Occurs
to her.*) What was it like?

GERDA: Repetitive. Crude. He has no imagination. And
he's not my Anatole.

WIDOW: Oh, my hair. (*A few strands of it are undone.*) That
blessed comb. I'm sure he has it.

GERDA: Use this. (*Holds out the carpet comb.*)

WIDOW: There's no need for you to he vulgar.

GERDA: (*Resumes combing.*) At least the carpet is its original
colour. I don't expect dandelion dye would stay fast in a
carpet. Mind you don't go out in the rain.

WIDOW: Gerda, you should show more respect. You never
know when you'll need me. (*Looks round anxiously,
Quietly, but firmly.*) Don't be influenced. Do you hear?
You were always wayward.

GERDA: You think I'll denounce you?

WIDOW: Don't be so impulsive. I'm not saying that at all.
You are too good a German, I know.

GERDA: (*Viciously.*) Like you.

WIDOW: What do you mean?

GERDA: You are so good a German as to tell on your
friends behind their backs. Like a squeaking schoolgirl,
except the punishment for me was a little more than a
ruler across the knuckles.

WIDOW: Don't exaggerate. You never got anything worse
than a reprimand.

GERDA: A beating. And for nothing.

WIDOW: For nothing? Do you call going to communist
meetings nothing?

GERDA: All of us went.

WIDOW: Speak for yourself. Intellectuals, perhaps.

GERDA: Not your husband?

WIDOW: Not as late as that. (*Changes tack.*) I heard you talking. The Red Front, a workers' militia, cells, propaganda...

GERDA: (*Tests her.*) Not with Franz.

WIDOW: Oh yes. That afternoon in the Walden Park. You thought I met you there on the path. You'd been sitting together on the bench by the lake. Well, I was sitting on the bench behind.

GERDA: Very clever. But what were we saying?

(*The WIDOW doesn't answer.*)

You see? It turned out there was nothing in it, didn't it?

WIDOW: How was I to know? Two intellectuals only giving their brains an airing! And he being...so high.

GERDA: So high? Yes.

WIDOW: I only reported what I heard.

GERDA: (*Relieved.*) Yes, you did. (*Gets up, throws the comb down.*) The bitch on heat runs to the first dog that'll take her.

WIDOW: You were never such a bitch.

GERDA: What?

WIDOW: Didn't you accuse my husband?

GERDA: (*Goes to window as if on guard.*) No, I said he was in the Social Democratic Party. Well, he was.

WIDOW: You didn't stop at that. You brought up the subject of a certain speech he gave to a party meeting. Remember?

GERDA: We all spoke against the Brownshirts then. Why mention it now?

WIDOW: But we didn't all say they should be locked up.

GERDA: Luckily your husband proved to be invaluable. In two years he knew the race laws inside out.

WIDOW: Whereas your husband continued his work as a Bolshevik and a Jew.

GERDA: (*Laughs shrilly, hysterically.*) If only he'd been either!

WIDOW: Fetch me the towel.

(*GERDA fetches the towel from the toilet. Enter PETKA,
furtively. He is drunk. The women cringe.*)

(*To GERDA, in a whisper.*) The carpet!

(*But PETKA immediately takes GERDA to one side. The
WIDOW perfunctorily dries her feet.*)

PETKA: (*Looks towards the door, in a low voice.*) Do me a
favour, dear lady.

GERDA: Another one?

(*They go to the window. The WIDOW, bare-footed, urgently
rolls up the carpet.*)

PETKA: (*In undertone, politely.*) Please. It is the question of a
girl. It's May Day. You understand? She must be clean
and decent, she must be good, affectionate... Plenty of
bread. Bacon, if she's very good.

GERDA: (*Stares at PETKA, bursts out laughing.*) Well, well.
Good, clean and affectionate. You're asking a lot. You
wouldn't like her to have a doctor's certificate as well,
would you? No, Petka, it's impossible. I know very few
women round here and they are old and ugly. (*PETKA is
very disappointed.*) Not good enough for a young boy like
you. (*Pats him on the cheek.*) Cheer up.

(*PETKA, from nowhere, pulls out a pair of silk stockings and
dangles them in GERDA's face.*)

PETKA: You want? I give you.

GERDA: You pig. (*Turns her back on him.*)

PETKA: You want bacon. I get bacon.

GERDA: I have bacon.

(*Enter ANATOLE, happy, only a little drunk. PETKA hides
the stockings.*)

(*Quickly.*) Anatole, tell him not to be stupid.

ANATOLE: Petka, don't be stupid.

(*PETKA demurs, but sees the WIDOW's feet. The WIDOW
is caught standing on a chair trying to shove the carpet away
on top of the cupboard.*)

PETKA: (*To the WIDOW.*) I am a young man. I am healthy.
It will be over in no time. (*Rolls his eyes.*) I'm good. You
will see. (*Clenches his fists. Kneels. Whispers to the
WIDOW's feet.*) It's a big one.

(*The WIDOW turns and kicks him away. PETKA grabs her by the legs, angrily, pulling her off the chair. ANATOLE laughs.*)

What of it? Your husband is not here. What's the matter? Don't you like me? (*To GERDA.*) Doesn't she like Petka?

GERDA: Oh yes, she likes you.

PETKA: Well then, you tell her. Tell her Petka is good. You know he is. Petka hasn't had a woman today. It's bad. Tell her it's very bad. She will understand.

(*The WIDOW is rigid with terror.*)

GERDA: Anatole, you tell her.

ANATOLE: (*Laughing, looks at GERDA, then at WIDOW.*) Quite right. It's not important. You persuade her, Gerda. It won't last long and she can cry afterwards. Tell her not to take it to heart.

PETKA: (*To ANATOLE.*) What did you say? (*To GERDA.*) Tell her she is beautiful. Tell her Russian women – like this. (*Forms a large circle with both thumbs and forefingers.*) German women – like this. (*Forms a small circle with one thumb and forefinger.*)

GERDA: (*To WIDOW.*) He says you are beautiful. He worships you. You'd better have him. He's got big fists too.

ANATOLE: (*Laughs.*) She'll understand. (*To the WIDOW, bitterly.*) Take a holiday, dear Frau. It's Labour Day. The workers are celebrating. Why not enjoy it?

(*The WIDOW cries. PETKA, pacified, strokes her.*)

PETKA: Come along, lady. Don't mind your face. I think it's beautiful. At least, today it is. Have a taste of my bacon. I bet it's been a long time, eh! You have been waiting for love. Ah! I understand. Come along, dear Frau. I know a little corner. You will like it. You'll see.

WIDOW: At least let me put on my shoes. (*Searches for her shoes.*)

PETKA: What?

GERDA: Her shoes.

PETKA: (*Angrily.*) Her shoes! What does it matter about her shoes! (*Waits rudely, impatiently.*)

ANATOLE: (*Can't contain it any longer.*) Gerda, Berlin is surrendering in the morning! Our flag flies over the Reichstag. Hitler has killed himself.

PETKA: (*Gestures excitedly.*) Berlin kaputt. Gitler kaputt, Goebbels kaputt. Stalin goot!

(*The WIDOW pauses, stunned. She and GERDA look at each other.*)

WIDOW: Are you telling the truth?

ANATOLE: Don't doubt us, dear Frau. It's nearly over!

GERDA: (*To WIDOW.*) Aren't you proud? The Germans are very brave. They fought to the last woman.

WIDOW: I don't understand. Where are the tanks?

ANATOLE: (*Laughs.*) Tanks?

WIDOW: Reinforcements are coming.

ANATOLE: Reinforcements! Schoolboys. No, there's nothing left. You have only the future, a clean slate. If you look back, you'll see nothing. Come along, dear Frau, even you should look up! Be cheerful! You're alive!

WIDOW: (*To GERDA.*) What did you say? (*Wanders, finds her shoes vaguely.*)

GERDA: (*Laughs.*) Yes, she's in a bit of a daze.

ANATOLE: Huh! She's quite stupid. But why? She's rich. She should be educated like you. (*The WIDOW slips on her shoes but does not tie the laces.*)

PETKA: There! You have your shoes. Now come! It's not so bad. (*Relishes the word 'Frau'.*) Dear Frau! You will see.

WIDOW: (*Indicates suitcase.*) Gerda. My things. (*Goes with PETKA.*)

ANATOLE: Another fine bourgeoise meets her redeemer.

GERDA: Why are you back so soon?

ANATOLE: It's a holiday. Meetings. Only a little business. We hurried home to learn from our betters. Is she very rich?

GERDA: (*Laughs.*) She's not rich. Her husband was a solicitor, quite well off, but altogether a minor character. Never made it in the Party. Never rose higher in the legal business. She was only a shopkeeper's daughter. They paid for her at high school but she didn't learn much. Naturally, she finds the present history lesson rather overwhelming.

ANATOLE: (*Laughs, sits at table.*) Ah! The Germans! So complicated. You clever! She stupid! Both eat well.

GERDA: Not Germans. The bourgeoisie. We all gave the Führer the children. The working women in the factories gave him the guns. We ate well, they got TB.

ANATOLE: So what are you going to do? Change the world?

GERDA: (*With heavy sarcasm.*) Change the world? Yes! Everyone changes the world, whatever he does. The Nazis changed the world. What world? What change?

ANATOLE: There's only one change.

GERDA: Towards socialism? Which socialism?

ANATOLE: Which socialism?

GERDA: (*Goes to window.*) When I was sixteen I wore an old-fashioned school uniform and argued for God because our teachers were Prussian nationalists. One day the history teacher suffered a stroke. His replacement was a young woman with short hair who called Frederick the Great an adventurer and the Social Democratic Reich President Ebert a great statesman. She would gaze at us with sparkling dark eyes and implore us, 'Girls! Try to change the world! It needs it!'

ANATOLE: There you are, you see.

GERDA: Not really. It was 1930. The Reichstag elections were being held. She took us to meetings of all the political parties. (*Approaches ANATOLE at the table.*) We worked our way through the National Socialists via the Centre and Democrats to the Socialists and Communists. When we were with the Nazis we saluted Hitler, and when we attended communist meetings we let ourselves be addressed as comrades. After ten days we gave up. (*Leaves table.*) We felt they were all horsetrading. It was all haggling, political jobbery, wrangling for power. No party seemed clean to us. We found it impossible to accept any one of them unconditionally. I think we should, then and there, have founded a new party – the party of the sixteen-year-olds, a clean party. But of course that would only have lasted for a year. (*Sits in armchair.*)

ANATOLE: Well, why didn't you do what your young
teacher said?

GERDA: Change the world? The world is changing and I'm
part of that change. I admit I can influence it. This little
me can make quite a difference. Depending on how I
decide to act, a man is frustrated or satisfied, a baby is
born or not born, a job of work I do is done my way. But
how I decide depends on all sorts of things, most of them
outside my control. If they are electing the Reichstag, I
will elect the Reichstag. If they are manufacturing
armaments, I will manufacture armaments. If they are
losing the war, I will lose the war. Did you ever hear of
anyone declaring peace all by themselves? Inside that
small space the sum of tears remains constant. Whether
Ebert is elected President or Hitler is Führer I will cry at
things that make me cry and laugh at things that make
me laugh. When I had too much to eat I still felt pain.
Now I have too little, I'm not crying from dawn to dusk
and some things still make me happy.

ANATOLE: (*Stands.*) You don't know the half of it.
(*Approaches GERDA.*) A person really starved is ground
down, their senses become dulled and they can't feel pain
or joy. Someone facing the SS firing squad in a
Ukrainian village won't thank you if you insist that
because the sky is blue that day, the sun shines and the
birds are singing, he should feel happy.

GERDA: Won't he? (*Gets up, restlessly.*) Then there's
something lacking in him. (*Goes to window.*) A woman
who gives birth is always near to death. It's agony. But if
she doesn't also feel joy, then she isn't capable of feeling
agony either.

ANATOLE: (*Beside the table.*) So you don't think there's any
difference between the murderer and his victim?

GERDA: (*At the window.*) Yes, there's a difference, of course.
But the similarities are greater. There are differences
between Communism, Parliamentarianism and Nazism.
Even considerable differences. But they are differences of
emphasis, of form and colour, minor modifications in the
rules of the game. If you are submissive, you will submit
in Moscow, London or Berlin. If you oppress, you will

oppress. If you resist, you will resist. I wouldn't like to live in Moscow. When I was there I couldn't stand the incessant ideological education. I like travel and Russians can't travel. There was a complete absence of erotic life, no fashions, no make-up, no stimulation. The regime didn't suit my temperament. Whereas London and Paris I got caught up in – fast, bright. Cities of illusions and despair. But I was always aware of being an outsider, a German. (*Approaches table.*) I returned to Germany of my own free will. Many of my friends advised me to emigrate. But I'm glad I came back. (*Beside the table.*) I feel I belong to my country, I'm determined to share its fate. The red flag was very attractive to me when I was younger. But nothing draws me to it now. (*Sits at table.*) As for Christian belief, I lost that even earlier – when I grew up and attained the age of reason!

ANATOLE: (*Moves away.*) Then there is no development, no progress?

GERDA: Yes, towards bigger bombs.

ANATOLE: And happiness? Isn't it worth pursuing?

GERDA: Who for? For Petka and the likes of him? Yes. But he seems to feel quite happy already.

ANATOLE: And wealth, prosperity – for your country, for yourself?

GERDA: Don't make me laugh. I've had a house, furniture, even a car. Now look at me – (*Picks up a piece of bacon.*) bombed out, homeless, bartering a body for a bone to suck. And you talk to me of creature comforts! (*Drops the meat.*)

ANATOLE: (*Sits at table, opposite GERDA.*) Finally, in this fascinating examination, your teacher will put down a question about love. Does it exist? Or is it, too, starved, blasted?

GERDA: Love? You obviously haven't understood. It is all because of love. Does a lover kill his rival because he hates him? No, it's because he loves her. Do you think Hitler kills Jews because he hates them? It's because he loves Aryans. You haven't conquered Germany because you hate Nazism, but because you love communism. You don't curse Germany because you hate the German people. You curse us because you love Russia. If you don't understand that, you're a very poor examiner and you have no right to ask me questions.

ANATOLE: (*Angrily.*) You seem to me to be delivering an implacable judgement, from a justice so rigorous, so objective, it becomes terrible, inhuman, unjust.

GERDA: Yes. Such truth is unjust. Does that frighten you?

ANATOLE: It might frighten me if I believed it. Don't play with me, Gerda. In your whole attitude you treat me as an inferior. I am uncultivated. But I'm not stupid. You say we haven't conquered Germany because we hate Nazism but because we love communism. That is very naive. Do we love communism? Then why should so many Ukrainians join the German army when they invaded us, why did they fight with them and serve them as puppets? You say you didn't like Moscow. The ideology was too strict. But it is not strict enough for some – Stakhanovites, dam-builders, Communist Youth, the young bloods in the political department of the Army. There was no sex, no stimulus for you. But some women find labour heroes quite stunning. And the sight of an open-faced, healthy girl, brown from the sun and air of the steppes, swinging a spade over her shoulder and marching off with her comrades to dig new fields – well, for some of our men it is rather more arousing than an advertisement for silk stockings. You say you like travel and Russians can't go abroad. Well, you see me here, don't you? What takes a person abroad? Either a train ticket or a soldier's pass. For the ticket he needs money. For the pass he needs youth and strength. For both he needs authority. Who will give him that authority? Wealth? The money of his class? Or power? The power of his class? Your German workers took the soldier's pass because they didn't have the money for the train ticket. But their holidays in the east were financed by the German bourgeoisie, so they proved brief and bloody. Now it's our turn to take a break in Berlin. As our passes are issued by the Russian proletariat, we're likely to stay for some time.

GERDA: So you do believe in love!

ANATOLE: I believe in the love of my class and in hatred for those opposed to it. I don't believe there is a love higher than that, a love that transcends classes. A worker may fall in love with someone from the bourgeoisie. But for that, the one will have to accept the life of the other, either the life of the worker or the life of the bourgeois. There is no universal love or hatred. The sum of tears is not constant. Something that makes you cry, when it happens to me, may give me joy. If you and I went to the May Day celebrations together, I would see you frown, you'd feel humiliated, but you'd see my face light up with happiness and pride.

GERDA: (*Relentlessly.*) And afterwards, after the march past, you would take me behind a shed. And in that act, in the same act, I would feel revulsion and you would find pleasure.

ANATOLE: That is class hatred.

GERDA: (*Precisely.*) Or dog love.

(*ANATOLE looks at her. They laugh, he with surprise, she with suppressed hysteria.*)

ANATOLE: You understand better than I do.

GERDA: It's strange to have a serious conversation with a man. The men I knew treated me as a little woman who had to be given a lecture before she understood.

ANATOLE: Even though you're educated?

GERDA: (*Bitterly.*) Especially as I'm educated. The German bourgeois resented me all the more because he suspected I knew as much as he did and maybe more.

ANATOLE: Even Franz?

GERDA: (*Emotionally.*) Yes, even Franz. He's nice, he's kind, but when it came to anything he regarded as important, he always knew best. It's different for you here. You listen to what I say. (*Angrily.*) But at home you don't speak to your wife as you speak to me. You shout and give orders and the little woman will wash the baby in the tub and see you have clean underwear.

ANATOLE: You understand...even at this distance...without going there! We had a socialist equality movement when

the collective farms came. The women were set free of
the home. But now I look at it, that only meant they
worked on the farm alongside us. At home, things didn't
change very much. Though I haven't heard it expressed
quite like that before.

GERDA: (*With something like hysteria.*) You had to come all
the way to Berlin to hear it. What a lot of trouble you
took! (*Suddenly.*) Have you any decent soap?

ANATOLE: Soap? No, I don't think I have.

GERDA: (*Cries out.*) How I want to scrub my skin, scrub it
till it shines!

(*ANATOLE stands, goes to the door, turns back into the room.*)

ANATOLE: What do you think of us Bolshevik barbarians?

GERDA: (*With heavy sarcasm.*) I'm not impressed. You are
not like Berliners. I don't want to be unfair. Obviously I
haven't met your best troops. When I do, ask me again.

ANATOLE: (*Laughs.*) Our 'best troops'? Surely you realised.
We are them. (*Bows.*) Dear lady, the signals and
intelligence corps – at your service. The elite. We were
sent into this district purposely – to impress the Berlin
bourgeoisie. No, I hope you don't meet our ordinary
troops. The transport columns reek of horse dung. The
infantry are filthy, listless, moronic. I don't know where
they dig them up. I'm sure there's nothing like them
even in Molotov. No, better not meet them, Gerda. If you
want to keep your illusions. (*Abruptly.*) Will you work
with us?

GERDA: (*Though this is not unexpected.*) You are too blunt.
Ask me nicely.

ANATOLE: Nicely? Well, how shall I put it? You know I've
become exactly the military type. (*Tries.*) Stalin has
decreed all women with a Russian child are to be given a
Ration Card Grade One. (*Pause.*)

GERDA: That's better. How much?

ANATOLE: Six hundred grams of bread a day, one hundred
grams of meat. And coffee beans. You will be in good
company. Managers, technicians, doctors, clergymen,
'notable artists' – they all have Ration Card Grade One.

GERDA: The same mixture. I'd rather do myself in.

ANATOLE: Then you are content on Grade Five with 'the
remaining population' – those who do no productive

work? Three hundred grams of bread, twenty grams of meat. And no coffee. Of course, you can aspire to Grade One without going to the trouble of having a child.

GERADA: Oh yes?

ANATOLE: Just report tomorrow at eleven at the City Hall. You will say you have experience in 'cultural activities'. We call our newspapers 'culture', you know.

GERDA: Like washing your hands.

ANATOLE: Like washing our hands. Well? (*Pause.*) Bring your identity card. You'll have to turn it in for a new one. There's a long list of names already, working for the new municipal authority. They want to start a paper, 'New Action'.

GERDA: Who are they?

ANATOLE: Emigrés. Returned from Moscow.

GERDA: But you know my position

ANATOLE: That is no barrier. At the very least, they'll assign you work as an interpreter.

GERDA: Will they help me find Franz?

ANATOLE: Franz? Yes. If you still want to. Or we can do it. (*Enter the WIDOW, alone. She has lost a shoe. Her face is bloody. She is pale, dusty, dishevelled. She goes to her armchair and half falls into it. GERDA goes to her.*)

WIDOW: My shoe. I can't think where... (*Her voice trails away.*)

GERDA: It'll be all right. (*Silence.*)

ANATOLE: (*Bitterly.*) You see, it wasn't so bad.

GERDA: Get her a cloth.

(*ANATOLE fetches a cloth from the toilet. GERDA bathes the WIDOW's face and forehead.*)

It's all right.

WIDOW: Where can it be?

ANATOLE: Where's Petka?

WIDOW: My best walking pair.

ANATOLE: Where is he?

WIDOW: Who?

ANATOLE: Petka.

WIDOW: The soldier-boy? He's gone. Gone away.

ANATOLE: Gone where? What do you mean?

WIDOW: I don't know.

ANATOLE: (*To GERDA.*) He'll be replenishing himself. A tougher assignment than he expected. (*To WIDOW.*) We were talking about the future, dear Frau.

WIDOW: (*Near to breaking.*) What?

ANATOLE: The future. What will you do?

WIDOW: Me? Do? You ask me now? (*Near to breaking. Looks at GERDA. Covers up.*) I can't be sure. They guaranteed me my husband's life insurance.
(*ANATOLE laughs.*)
I may have to work.
(*ANATOLE laughs more loudly.*)

ANATOLE: What can you do?

GERDA: She has money in the bank.

WIDOW: (*Recovers.*) Gerda, it is not red money.

ANATOLE: (*Takes cloth.*) You have blood on your hands. (*Wipes her hands.*) Don't worry. All money is tainted. They'll let you have it.

WIDOW: (*Takes another tack.*) You are very kind. What gentlemen Russian officers are! I can cook.

ANATOLE: Cook! (*Laughs.*) We can cook! Isn't there something you can do for us? Something we don't know?

WIDOW: (*Uncertainly.*) Well. I did my husband's book-keeping.

ANATOLE: Ah! Yes, yes. Anything else? What about a nice clean German laundry?

WIDOW: I have to be careful of my hands.

ANATOLE: You could manage it. Organise the washer-women!

WIDOW: Well, I might.

ANATOLE: There are a lot of uniforms could do with a scrubbing.

WIDOW: (*Brightens.*) Uniforms?

ANATOLE: What a noble task! Mud, blood, sick, sweat. You would see how we won our victory.

WIDOW: (*Downcast.*) Russian uniforms.

ANATOLE: In time for the victory celebrations. Set yourself up. A little business. What do you think?

WIDOW: (*Flattered.*) Well, I've always been an independent-minded person.

ANATOLE: So you like the idea! I'll put your name forward.

WIDOW: The gentleman is very kind. (*Near to breaking.*) I have no one left in the world. (*Breaks down.*)

GERDA: What is it? What's happened?

WIDOW: Gerda.

GERDA: Tell me.

WIDOW: I killed him.

GERDA: You what?

WIDOW: He threw me on the ground. He opened my mouth with his two hands and...dribbled. Into my mouth. Thick green phlegm. I squeezed him. Between two bricks. I didn't let go. He roared and fell off. I got up. I hit him in the eye. With a bar. An iron railing. He fell down. I hit him. On the head. With a stone. Again... and again...

GERDA: (*Slaps the WIDOW hard on the face.*) You're stupid! (*Turns away in disgust.*)

WIDOW: I had to, Gerda.

GERDA: Stupid heroics. You silly bitch. You really don't understand.

ANATOLE: (*Diffidently.*) Even now, she doesn't understand. (*Laughs.*) It must be the language barrier.

GERDA: (*To ANATOLE.*) Yes! Shall we teach her a bit of Russian?

ANATOLE: (*Laughs.*) Of course. What shall it be? 'Ssozialistitscheski'?

GERDA: (*Considers.*) That's a bit beyond her.

ANATOLE: 'Ssamo-Ubitschestwo'?

GERDA: (*Laughs.*) Suicide? That's going to the other extreme. How about 'Druzhba'?

ANATOLE: (*Claps.*) Druzhba! That's right!

GERDA: (*To the WIDOW, as to an idiot.*) Now! We're going to teach you a little Russian, 'Druzhba'. Can you say it?

WIDOW: What?

GERDA Say, 'Druzhba'.

WIDOW: Druzhba.

ANATOLE: Ah!

GERDA: Very good.

WIDOW: What does it mean?

GERDA: It means 'Friendship'.

(*Pause.*)

ANATOLE: Well! (*Looks around.*) Well, Gerda. Shall we see
what's on for May Day?

GERDA: (*Laughs. Quietly.*) Won't you turn her in?

ANATOLE: (*Quietly to GERDA.*) Is it as she says?

GERDA: (*Bitterly.*) She wouldn't lie. Not about that.

ANATOLE: (*Loudly.*) We can say a wall fell on him. (*Quietly
to GERDA.*) She'll still be here.

WIDOW: (*To GERDA.*) Are you going?

(*GERDA is deliberating.*)

There's a notice.

ANATOLE: What?

WIDOW: (*To ANATOLE.*) A new notice.

GERDA: Oh? What does it say?

WIDOW: (*With the full force of her hatred.*) 'Russians are
forbidden from houses inhabited by Germans. Or to
have any dealings with German civilians.'

ANATOLE: Yes. About time.

GERDA: They're learning. (*To ANATOLE.*) Who is it?

(*Collects a few things together.*)

ANATOLE: The military commission.

WIDOW: (*To GERDA.*) Don't go. Are you going?

GERDA: Of course.

ANATOLE: (*Laughs, then hums, and sings.*) 'Oh stay and
linger, my beloved!'

WIDOW: (*Screams.*) She's a Nazi. Don't you know? Her
Franz is a Gruppenführer. In the SS. She betrayed you.
Years ago.

GERDA: (*Screams.*) You bitch. (*Goes for the WIDOW.*)

WIDOW: You're the bitch. Don't you see? She's a lying
bitch! A bitch and a whore!

ANATOLE: (*Carefully.*) Dear Frau. Please.

GERDA: (*Screams.*) Who betrayed? You did. You betrayed
me. You betrayed everyone you could. (*Goes for her.*)

WIDOW: (*Screams.*) She's a Red. She always was. She
denounced my husband. Curse you. You Jew. She's a Jew.
The reptile. She's poison. Poison in the blood.

(*She makes a stab at GERDA with her shoe, ANATOLE
pulls her off.*)

ANATOLE: I must ask you... (*Quietly.*) You're too excited.
(*Pushes her on to a chair.*) Why? Don't make a fool of
yourself, dear Frau.
(*The WIDOW is utterly deflated.*)
WIDOW: (*Clamours, pleads.*) Give me my money.
ANATOLE: You'll get your money.
WIDOW: Let me have it. It's only a few thousand. You will
set me up in business, won't you? You'll see I'm all
right?
ANATOLE: You'll be all right. I assure you we will pay
careful attention to your needs. A lively tongue like
yours – and ambition – how can you fail?
(*The WIDOW is silent, numbed, stupefied, uncomprehending.*
ANATOLE clicks his heels, bows mockingly.)
(*Suddenly.*) Doswidanja.
WIDOW: (*Automatically.*) Doswidanja.
ANATOLE: (*Smirks.*) She can say that too!
WIDOW: What does it mean?
GERDA: 'Good-bye.' (*Looks around, glances at the flat.*) Well.
Doswidanja!
(*No reply. The WIDOW sinks lower into the chair. GERDA*
and ANATOLE go out together. The WIDOW reflects. She
stands. She feels inside her skirt, pulls out the ring attached
to her elastic. It glints golden. She holds it, gripped. She wonders
whether to detach it. She decides to return it to where it was.
Does so. Looks around. Goes to the window, looks out.)
WIDOW: Doswidanja. (*Reflects. Looks up.*) I wonder what's
'Hello'?
(*From outside comes the sound of May Day celebrations. Lorries,*
tanks, shouts, cheers. A radio broadcast of a speech, a Russian
army march. Finally, the first lines of the Internationale,
not, this time, on an accordion but by a Red Army choir and
orchestra. The WIDOW stands listening at the window.)

PARTISANS

Days of Action

Characters

CINDY (*later* LUCIA) MUNDAY

HANS SCHNEIDER

RUTH

About 12 players are needed for the following parts:

FIRST FIGURE (Woman)

SECOND FIGURE (Man)

FIRST MAN

SECOND MAN

FIRST WOMAN

AIR-RAID WARDEN

PROVO

CYCLIST

HERBIE

JEZZ

PASSERS-BY

PRIVATE JOHN WAIN

FILM CAMERAMAN

BAR-OWNER

MRS SHITE

PRIVATE ENTERPRISE

TV CAMERAMAN

TV CAMERAMAN'S ASSISTANT

JUDGE

CLERK OF THE COURT

COUNSEL FOR THE PROSECUTION

PSYCHIATRIST

COUNSEL FOR THE DEFENCE

PRESS PHOTOGRAPHERS

JEAN-LUC GODARD

STUDENTS

The Aldershot Brigade:

LESZEK

CLAUDIA

PAUL

WINSTON

SAS MEN

TV CAMERA CREW

REPORTER

MAN WARDER

WOMAN WARDER

ARCHBISHOP OF CANTERBURY

ATTENDANT

TWO STRONG MEN

The Prologue takes place in May 1941. The remainder of the play takes place between 1966 and 1982.

House music, to be played before and after the play and in the interval: Joy Division's 'She's Lost Control' (*Unknown Pleasures*, Fac 10), 'Love will tear us apart' (single, Fac 23), 'Atrocity Exhibition' (*Closer*, Fac 25).

The author acknowledges the inspiration from Tuli Kupferberg for *Fucknam* and from Roger Howard for 'Dis' (*New Short Plays,* Methuen, 1968).

Prologue

A bare stage. May 1941. London's East End. Night. Bombers overhead. Searchlights. Some anti-aircraft fire. Bombs exploding. Fires. Dim shapes of a group of people who have taken cover, most of them lying prone. A bomb, whistling. A loud explosion. The FIGURE of a woman, lying centre stage. Anti-aircraft fire. A SECOND FIGURE, a man, crawls towards the first. The bombers pass. Fires. The SECOND FIGURE slowly stands, holding a baby. The FIRST FIGURE remains on the ground. The prone figures slowly rise and gather round the SECOND FIGURE.

FIRST MAN: Cor blimey!

SECOND MAN: Bleedin' 'ell. (*Touches baby.*)

FIRST MAN: Gift from 'Itler.

SECOND MAN: All bloody sticky.

(*Two WOMEN examine the baby.*)

FIRST WOMAN: Is it all right?

SECOND WOMAN: She'll be cold. (*Offers shawl.*)

FIRST WOMAN: Poor little thing.

SECOND WOMAN: Needs washin'. (*Takes baby.*)

SECOND MAN: Look out.

(*AIR-RAID WARDEN in tin helmet enters, brushing off dust.*)

WARDEN: I thought this street had trekked off to Eppin' bleedin' Forest like last time. What's the bleedin' row?

FIRST MAN: Can't keep us down, can yer?

WARDEN: (*To FIRST MAN.*) 'Ere, I know you. You're the one what bloody cries alert at four in the afternoon so you can get to the bleedin' tube shelter before the rush.

FIRST MAN: No I ain't, cock.

SECOND MAN: Bloody shirker.

FIRST WOMAN: Eppin' Forest? What about me little uns' clothing allowance? No bloody address there.

WARDEN: (*Sees baby.*) Blimey.

FIRST WOMAN: It's 'ers. I got enough of me own. (*To SECOND FIGURE.*) What yer gonna call it?

SECOND FIGURE: It's 'ers.

(*They see the corpse.*)

FIRST WOMAN: Gawd!

SECOND WOMAN: Chris'.

FIRST MAN: Bloody 'ell. (*Begins to make off.*)

SECOND MAN: Bloody 'ead sliced off.

SECOND WOMAN: Chris' almighty.

FIRST WOMAN (*To SECOND FIGURE.*) Are you 'er 'usband?

SECOND WOMAN: 'O are you?

SECOND FIGURE: Never seen 'er before. (*Begins to go.*)

FIRST MAN: Bloody 'ell. (*Goes.*)

SECOND WOMAN: 'Ere. (*Gives baby to WARDEN. Makes off.*)

(*They all make off leaving the WARDEN.*)

WARDEN: 'Ere you! (*Looks around. Puts baby on the ground. Goes.*)

(*Empty stage. First light. The SECOND WOMAN returns. Looks around. Goes to the baby. Kneels, touches her. Picks her up. Talks to her. Walks with her. The SECOND FIGURE returns. He is a worker wearing an overcoat. He carries a rifle.*)

SECOND WOMAN: What do you want?

SECOND FIGURE: What?

SECOND WOMAN: Are you the father?

SECOND FIGURE: Blimey no.

SECOND WOMAN: Well then? (*Pause.*)

SECOND FIGURE: Are you gonna take it?

SECOND WOMAN: Take it?

SECOND FIGURE: Are you gonna look after it?

SECOND WOMAN: What's that to you? (*Pause.*)

SECOND FIGURE: Are you?

SECOND WOMAN: It's gonna need some bleedin' milk, init? (*Pause.*) What was she to you?

SECOND FIGURE: Nothin'. (*Pause.*) I worked with 'er.

SECOND WOMAN: What?

SECOND FIGURE: In the factory. On the line. Makin' bombs.

SECOND WOMAN: Bombs! Gawd. (*Pause.*) You know 'er, then.

SECOND FIGURE No. Jus' saw 'er. Across the line.

SECOND WOMAN: Well, 'o's 'er 'usband then?

SECOND FIGURE Didn't 'ave one.

SECOND WOMAN: Didn't 'ave one! Bloody 'ell. We're bloody caught now, ain't we?

SECOND FIGURE: Who is?

SECOND WOMAN: We're in the bleedin' soup.

(*Dawn spreads. The all-clear sounds. The SECOND FIGURE looks at the sky. The AIR-RAID WARDEN approaches. The SECOND FIGURE conceals his rifle under his overcoat. The WARDEN sums up the situation.*)

WARDEN: (*Rubs his hands.*) Yes, well. (*Looks at sky, at ruins.*) Not too bad, was it?

(*The WARDEN nods to them and goes. The SECOND WOMAN opens her blouse to the girl. Freeze.*)

1: The White Pig Plan

Summer 1966. Unfreeze. It is CINDY. She was playing her foster-mother, the baby was CINDY.

CINDY: 'I came into the world at a time of disorder.'

(*She throws the 'baby' off. The SECOND FIGURE goes off. CINDY addresses the audience.*)

I sometimes have your dream. I'm walking down the street. It's deserted. Suddenly I stop by a concrete wall. I run my hand along it. I think, 'There's ten minutes left. When I go, this wall will go too. It won't be there. It'll turn into vapour, disintegrate. No-one will be there to see.'

(*Enter PROVO in a white coat, on a journey.*)

PROVO: (*To CINDY.*) The asphalt terror of the motorised bourgeoisie has lasted long enough. Human sacrifices are made daily to this latest idol of the idiots: car power. Choking carbon monoxide is its incense, its image contaminates thousands of streets. Our White Bicycle plan will liberate us from the car monster. The first White Bicycle will be presented to the Press and public today. The White Bicycle is never locked. The White Bicycle is the first free communal transport. The White

Bicycle can be used by anyone who needs it and then must be left for someone else. There will be more and more White Bicycles until everyone can use white transport and the car peril is past. The White Bicycle stands for simplicity and cleanliness in contrast to the vanity and foulness of the authoritarian car. City dwellers: a Bike is still Something, but it's very nearly Nothing!
(*A woman, dressed in white, enters on a white bicycle, pursued by PRESS PHOTOGRAPHERS.*)

CINDY: Excuse me.
(*The CYCLIST stops.*)
Did you see that?

CYCLIST: Did I see what?

CINDY: The wall there.

CYCLIST: What wall?

CINDY: You went right through that wall.
(*The CYCLIST looks around for the wall.*)

PROVO: (*To CYCLIST.*) Comrade, if you see a car letting off a cloud of poisonous gas, take its number and phone 862286 between four-thirty and five. We'll move into action right away.

CYCLIST: Thank you, comrade.

PROVO: (*Going.*) We know how to deal with noxious fumes.
(*Goes on his journey.*)

CYCLIST: Brmm, brmm. (*Gives a leaflet to CINDY.*) Don't drop this in the street. (*Cycles off, pursued by PHOTOGRAPHERS.*)

CINDY: (*Reads.*) 'We have formed a Society of Friends of the Police. We have one rule. All blue pigs must become white pigs. If this is difficult for some pigs, our suggestion is this. Start with the helmet. And also, white pigs carry aspirin in their pockets, a box of matches, an ounce or two of cannabis and apple sauce with a little pig steak. Why not have fun? White pig is good for you.'
(*Drops leaflet. To audience.*) Or sometimes the one where you're walking across a kind of open space, a field or a playground. You smell flesh burning – though you've never smelt burning flesh – and you see a child. Running towards you. Its hands stretched out.

2: Dialectics Of Liberation: A Peep Show

Summer 1967. CINDY and HERBIE, a Lancastrian with an American accent, converse in very confined quarters. Uptight male and female PASSERS-BY stop and view the relationship from outside through a peep-hole.

HERBIE: So you're twenty-five years old, on to heavy drugs, four months pregnant, your lover's gone. It's so corny it must be real. Afraid to ask for help from your momma and poppa. So you've got this friend, okay? He comes to see us. We just have to help you.

CINDY: I feel sick.

HERBIE: But, baby, if we don't help you, you'll be put in society, and faced with that you'll crash again, baby, you'll sure crash again.

CINDY: That's about where I am, Herbie.

HERBIE: You are, Cindy.

CINDY: I needed your crash pad real bad, Herbie.

HERBIE: You did, Cindy. People want pads, they want jobs, they want drugs. Lawyers, accountants, doctors, psychiatrists. We gottem. We got beds, we got typewriters, we got telephones.

CINDY: But I'm frightened of all that.

HERBIE: No, baby, you're not frightened of all that. I told you, we're love. We're the alternative to what frightens you, baby. We're the solution, you're the problem.

CINDY: I'm still frightened.

HERBIE: No, you're not frightened, honey. You're frightened of being frightened. Can I call Jezz now?

CINDY: Yeh, call Jezz. Who's Jezz?

HERBIE (*'Rings' Jezz on a 'phone'.*) A hard shrink, baby. Mainliner. Hi. Jezz. Can you come round? (*To CINDY.*) Where are we, honey?

CINDY: 54a Ladbroke Gardens.

HERBIE: She's 54a Ladbroke Gardens, Jezz. A hard rap. Love her, baby. Okay, Jezz. Love and peace. See yer. (*'Hangs up.'*) Be happy. It'll pass. I crashed like that in Berkeley.

CINDY: Yeh? I was born near Burnley.

HERBIE: Berkeley. Relax baby. All men are in chains. You won't be into that. Thousand dollars for a leather suit. Five hundred for a whip. You need bread, baby. There's the bondage of poverty. Dig that. The bondage of lust for power, status, possessions. I thought you said you were a Londoner.

CINDY: I got a cramp. (*Goes to 'window'.*)

HERBIE: It's the baby. Get rid of it. The arrogance of the father. Don't listen to him. A reign of terror is now perpetrated on a global scale.
(*CINDY looks out of the 'window'.*)
Vietnam, the Third World.

CINDY: The trash can needs emptying.

HERBIE: The whole of our affluent society is a con. The nuclear family is nuclear war. You're a hypothetical point on a dehumanised co-ordinate system.

CINDY: Hey, there's the rent man.

HERBIE: In total context, culture is against us, education enslaves us, technology kills us.

CINDY: Christ, he's coming up.

HERBIE: We must combat our self-pretended ignorance as to what goes on and our consequent non-reaction to what we refuse to know.

CINDY: What shall I do?

HERBIE What, baby?

CINDY: I owe a month.

HERBIE: The lunar pause. We're all moon crazy, man.

CINDY: But what should I do?

HERBIE: What is, is not the limit of what is possible. Show your non-acquisitiveness in a hostile acquisitive ambience. Pay up.

CINDY: The last dime went in the gas meter this morning,

HERBIE: Relax. Be my friend. It's part of the treatment.
(*Enter JEZZ, a black man, with a camera.*)
Cindy, Jezz. Inspirator of the New Community. Owns the block.

CINDY: I thought you were the rent man.

JEZZ: I'm the landlord.

CINDY: Christ.

JEZZ: Don't worry, be happy.

CINDY: I'll pay you next week.

JEZZ: Wah! What's the hurry?

CINDY: I've no bread and I thought...

JEZZ: Who's talking about bread? Such a lovely girl and I'm the Divine Loaf. I love you more than you can ever love yourself.

HERBIE: I told you.

JEZZ: Pour your drop into my ocean and become the ocean which in reality you are. We'd like you to get frocked. Men and women of all ages are joining our church in the holy search for Truth.

HERBIE: We love you, Cindy.

JEZZ: We worship God. That's our desire. The great need of the soul is that, Cindy. We do it in different ways. Herbie is Jewish. I'm a Buddhist. Mebbe you're a Christian. What does it matter? We gotta do something sacred. (*Takes angles on CINDY.*) The exodus from Egypt, that's Herbie's inner being. I'm into mantras. I'm immanent with crazy spirit exchanges. This pad of yours is going to stand your vibes all right, Cindy. (*Mesmerising.*) It's taking a wreck, no doubt about it. That's the best thing ever happened to you. Crashing here makes you strong enough to take all your love juice, Cindy. It's good here. Good in the strength of God. It's God's place, do you get that? Do you get my vibes? It's right here, an' it's going on getting better. (*CINDY takes up poses.*) Our place, Cindy. Our place for meditation. We believe in our minds, we believe in our bodies. (*Takes angles on CINDY.*) The place for consciousness-raising. A holy place, a place for wholeness. We confess here. Cindy, we have communion. This is the sacrament. Good in the strength of God. It goes on getting better, this place, it's sacred, Cindy, it's a sacred place, full of love. (*He has found his place.*)

HERBIE: (*To CINDY.*) You got a profoundly emotional death-rebirth there. Honey! You're chosen for God's work.

CINDY: How much?

(She begins to undress. The PASSERS-BY are well satisfied with what they are watching.)

3: Cindy Performs In 'Fucknam'

Summer 1967. A London arts laboratory performance before a counter-cultural audience.

Beethoven's Pastoral Symphony. CAPTAIN SHITE (played by SCHNEIDER), BAR-GIRL (played by CINDY).

CPT SHITE: *(Makes aircraft noises.)* Danang. Mekong Delta. Bay of Tonkin. Haiphong. Hanoi. Saigon. *(Makes bombing noises.)* Monday napalm. Tuesday napalm. Wednesday napalm. Thursday napalm. Friday napalm. Saturday napalm. Sunday holy napalm. Napalm. Made in USA. *(Sings. Tune, 'Let the Good Times Roll'.)*
Come on baby let the gook heads roll
Come on baby let it thrill your soul
Come on baby let the gook heads roll
Roll ten years long.
BAR-GIRL: *(Sings.)* Feel so good
When you shoot
Come on baby
Kill kill kill some more!
(Enter PRIVATE JOHN WAIN, a black man.)
(At door of bar. To SHITE.) Come in fine American boys. You like pussy, Captain Shite? Come in. Come in.
PVT WAIN: *(Whoops, drunk.)* I wanna get me a rockette. I wanna fuck me a rockette.
CPT SHITE: Fuckin gook creep. *(Hits BAR-GIRL.)* Gimme a coke.
(Enter BAR-OWNER, fusses round soldiers.)
OWNER: You gentlemen happy? Food okay? Drinks okay? *(To SHITE.)* Captain Shite, you like fucky fuck fuck or blow job?
PVT WAIN: Me like sucky suck suck. Om gonna get me a rockette. I wanna ride me home on a rockette. I wanna suck me a rockette.

OWNER: Okay okay. (*Signs to BAR-GIRL as she brings a coke.*)

(*Enter MRS SHITE carrying their baby.*)

CPT SHITE: Table for two.

OWNER Yessir!

CPT SHITE: (*Chucks baby under chin.*) Tootle tootle chubby chop chops.

(*BAR-OWNER has brought a table and two chairs. MRS SHITE puts baby on a chair.*)

PVT WAIN: (*To BAR-GIRL.*) Down, ya fuckin bitch.

(*BAR-GIRL gets on all fours. WAIN gets on his knees with his head up her dress.*)

CPT SHITE: (*Seated, to BAR-OWNER.*) Two steaks, fuckin gook twat.

(*BAR-OWNER goes.*)

(*Sings.*) Fighting soldiers from the sky

Fearless men who jump and die

Men who mean just what they say

The brave men of the Green Beret.

MRS SHITE: I'll have barbecue spare ribs.

CPT SHITE: (*Hits her face.*) Shut ya fuckin mouth. You're an Army wife.

MRS SHITE: I don't like steak.

CPT SHITE: (*Hits her face.*) Shut ya fuckin mouth.

(*PVT WAIN rides BAR-GIRL from the back.*)

PVT WAIN: Whoopee! (*Swings 'hat' around his head.*) Let's go let's go.

(*BAR-OWNER re-enters.*)

OWNER: No steak sir.

CPT SHITE: You get me a fuckin steak. (*Kicks OWNER.*)

OWNER: Yessir! (*Takes baby, goes.*)

MRS SHITE: I don't like fuckin steak.

CPT SHITE: You like this fuckin steak. (*Hits her face.*)

MRS SHITE: Fuck you. No fuckin pussy for you tonight.

PVT WAIN: Sing ya fuckin bitch, sing!

(*MRS SHITE sits at table, drums on table-top with her fingers. CPT SHITE watches PVT WAIN climax as BAR-GIRL sings.*)

BAR-GIRL: (*Sings.*) Burn baby burn

Burn baby burn

Burn like ya mother, burn
Burn like ya father, burn
Burn like ya sister, burn
Burn like ya brother, burn
Burn baby burn.
(*PVT WAIN shoots off, knocking BAR-GIRL off balance, falls on her in a heap.*)

CPT SHITE: (*Stands to attention, sings.*)
Silver wings upon their chest
These are men, America's best
Men who fight by night and day
Courage take from the Green Beret.
(*To BAR-GIRL.*) Hey fuckin gook pussy.

MRS SHITE: No ya fuckin don't.

CPT SHITE: Shut up you fat bitch.

MRS SHITE: You prick. I'll cut ya fuckin prick off.

CPT SHITE: You stuff ya cunt wiv fuckin concrete.
(*BAR-OWNER brings two steaks to the table.*)

MRS SHITE: I'll piss on ya fuckin steak.
(*CPT SHITE sees steak, sits at table.*)

CPT SHITE: Gemme some fried rice.

OWNER Yessir! Food okay? Drinks okay? (*Goes.*)

MRS SHITE: (*At table.*) Your dick's the smallest in the Tenth Brigade.

CPT SHITE: I'll shove this fork up your ass. I told you not to talk like this in public. (*They eat.*)

MRS SHITE: Where's Eldred? (*They look round. Screams.*) Christ! (*Drops her face in the meat, claws it, sobs.*)

CPT SHITE: (*Spits out mouthful.*) Fuckin gooks. (*Gets up.*) Wain.

PVT WAIN: Sir.

CPT SHITE: We're on a mission.

PVT WAIN: Yessir. (*Gets up, sways.*)

BAR-GIRL: (*Pleads.*) No burn no burn.
(*Enter PRIVATE ENTERPRISE with firebrands, one for PVT WAIN. Enter TV CAMERAMAN with equipment and ASSISTANT.*)

TV DUO: Okay set it up here right-o cap'n it's a great mission okay. (*They trip over their cables etc.*) Hold it, hold it, wanna use colour on this.

CPT SHITE: (*Directs operations.*) Private Enterprise.
(*ENTERPRISE readies himself to apply firebrand to roof of peasant hut.*)
Private Wain.
(*WAIN likewise, reeling.*)
TV DUO: Super mission cap'n, wanna capture super mission fuckin Cong. Strafe them creeps in the rice paddy daddy.
CPT SHITE: Christ will you hurry up I don't have all fuckin day I got four more villages to do.
TV DUO: Okay cap'n.
CPT SHITE: Go man go.
(*PVT ENTERPRISE and PVT WAIN apply the firebrands to the roofs of the peasant huts. Flames sweep the stage and the auditorium. 'Kill for Peace' by The Fugs mixes with the beginning of the choral section of Beethoven's Choral Symphony. The Fugs track gradually submits to the Beethoven. The chorus gets louder with the noise of jet screams, crackling of flames, wailing of peasants, whoopees of the Americans. BAR-OWNER watches glumly. BAR-GIRL, squatting on ground, rocks and moans. MRS SHITE claws at the meat, screaming. The TV camera turns.*)

4: Cindy Changes Her Name

CINDY: (*To audience.*) I dreamed I was in this shelter. A huge space with concrete walls and no light, just a dim glow. Gradually people came in. They walked stiffly, they didn't seem to know where they were going. They weren't injured but when I looked at them I saw they had no faces. The skin had come off, just flesh, bits hanging off. They walked straight, their hands stretched out in front of them. A huge crowd of them, men and women, old people, young people, but no children. They walked up and down, calling out. Calling out their names, not very loud but very clear. I could hear them but nobody else could or anyway they took no notice, just went on walking, up and down, calling out their names. (*Pause.*) I'm going to change my name. In China the Red Guards are doing it. A girl's called Pale Moon, she changes it to

Red Sun. Cindy! (*Consults a Dictionary of Names.*)
'Lucinda: seventeenth-century poetic version of Lucy,
q.v. Lucia, Lucy. From the Latin *lux*, meaning light. St
Lucia a virgin martyred at Syracuse under Diocletian.'
Huh! Had her eyes put out. Mm. Patroness of the blind.
Poor sod. Lucia. Yes. I'll have that.

5: Pillow Talk:
Do They Eat Babies Any More?

LUCIA and SCHNEIDER have been making love.

LUCIA: I've changed my name.

SCHNEIDER: I've changed my sex.

LUCIA: Yeah?

SCHNEIDER: Yeah.

LUCIA: Hans Schneideress?

SCHNEIDER: Schneiderin. I was born a male but to be
fully human that was only half of the business.

LUCIA: Don't you want to know my name?

SCHNEIDER: Cindy.

LUCIA: Lucia. She was a saint. Got blinded.

SCHNEIDER: Lucia. Yeah, I seen the brand name on a
match-box.

LUCIA: Do you always make fun of people? Captain Shite.

SCHNEIDER: Well then. Why did you change your name?

LUCIA: Cindy was stupid.

SCHNEIDER: Now you're Lucia, you're sensible.

LUCIA: It wasn't me, it was my name.

SCHNEIDER: Are you sure? I'm not a German tailor.

LUCIA: (*Laughs.*) Is that what Schneider means? A little
Jewish tailor? Where were you born? Auschwitz?

SCHNEIDER: Walthamstow. Do you mind? – don't make
me a Jew. A German is bad enough.

LUCIA: A German man.

SCHNEIDER: What did the women do? Commit suicide
in moral outrage?

LUCIA: The women resisted. In the factories. In their
homes. In bed. Medical work in the hospitals.

SCHNEIDER: They dissolved in tears and put the fuses on the bombs.

LUCIA: In Germany too?

SCHNEIDER: Of course. It was good money.

LUCIA: It was a man's war. What else could they do?

SCHNEIDER: What are you against? Men, or the state?

LUCIA: Men invented the state.

SCHNEIDER: Women submitted.

LUCIA: If women submit, okay. But don't call it nature.

SCHNEIDER: If it isn't nature, you're a good actress. Do you always act the whore?

LUCIA: No, I usually eat babies.

SCHNEIDER: You're talking about theatre. I'm talking about liberation.

LUCIA: 'Monday napalm, Tuesday napalm, Wednesday napalm... Don't fuck with me, babe, you're fuckin with fire.' Men all over.

SCHNEIDER: When the Pentagon takes over their brains.

LUCIA: They respond well.

SCHNEIDER: They haven't much choice.

LUCIA: Much? They have some. And throw it away.

SCHNEIDER: While you take your chances. Fuck all the way to the bank.

LUCIA: Yeah I do. I'm coming with you. I'm going to university.

SCHNEIDER: You what?

LUCIA: Do philosophy.

SCHNEIDER: Philosophy? An actress? The stage don't want brains when you got a cunt.

LUCIA: So what? I'm going somewhere better than 'Fucknam'.

6: The Old Bailey Soap Opera

Summer 1968. LUCIA and SCHNEIDER before a JUDGE.

JUDGE: In the case of Regina versus Schneider and Munday: the charge is incitement to assault. Will the clerk of the court read the offending article.

SCHNEIDER: Milud, may I request your democratic discretion? As no offence has yet been proved, will you amend your description to 'the alleged offending article'?

JUDGE: Very well. I can't see it makes any difference. Will the clerk of the court read the alleged offending article?

CLERK: The alleged article...

JUDGE: Not the alleged article. It's only alleged in the offending.

CLERK: The alleged offending is called...

JUDGE: Article.

CLERK: Article. The alleged offending is called article...

JUDGE: The alleged offending article.

CLERK: Yes, milud. The alleged offending article... It's a leaflet, milud.

JUDGE: Well the alleged offending leaflet. I can't see it makes any difference.

CLERK: The alleged offending leaflet is called 'The Use of Wall Newspapers'.

SCHNEIDER: Objection, judge. You are asking the clerk of the court to read a leaflet that is allegedly offending under a charge of incitement to assault. If the alleged offence is real, he may very well – especially with his voice which is so rich and authoritative – he may run the risk of inciting this court, milud, which as you can see is at fever pitch already and just waiting for the match to spark the fire. I propose, milud, in the interests of civil order to which as a good student I am democratically devoted, that you clear the court.

JUDGE: The court is exempt from influence of such a nature. Objection over-ruled. Proceed.

CLERK: The alleged offending leaflet is called 'The Use of Wall Newspapers'. I now read the document.
'Handwritten or duplicated newspapers should be established, in the form of poster-size sheets stuck on walls or boards, inside or outside buildings, at sites in factories, universities and streets convenient for people to stand and study their contents.
'Workers and students (or passers-by in the street) should be encouraged to answer, support or oppose the

established wall newspapers, not by replacing them or altering them but by adding their own contributions on separate adjacent sheets. Whether these additional sheets be single words or sentences or whole pages of argument, and whatever their content, the right to have them posted up must be respected. It will be in the hands of the democratic groups to ensure that in turn no reactionary statement goes unopposed.

'In the case of hard news, selection may be made according to democratic criteria. Comment on local and national news will present the democratic alternative to the capitalist orientated opinions put out by the official media. But the main purpose of wall newspapers is to DEVELOP CRITICAL ATTACKS ON ASPECTS OF THE WORK-PLACE WHERE THE WALL NEWSPAPER APPEARS, INCLUDING ASSAULTS ON INDIVIDUALS IN POSITIONS OF POWER.'

JUDGE: Thank you. Do I need a psychiatrist's report?

SCHNEIDER: I should say you do, judge. But I wouldn't trust them.

JUDGE: No laughter in court!

COUNSEL FOR THE PROSECUTION: The accused Schneider would not submit to psychiatric examination, milud. The accused Munday's report is here.

PSYCHIATRIST: I made a thorough physical and neurological examination of the accused. She first demanded a female practitioner, milud, but I explained she would be quite safe with me.

SCHNEIDER: He strips people of their self-esteem, that's all, milud.

PSYCHIATRIST: Lucia Munday is twenty-seven years old, of neurasthenic constitution. Her body is supple and of feminine proclivities.

JUDGE: A psychiatric report, please.

PSYCHIATRIST: Miss Munday is organically sound. But she shows marked nervous-vegetative symptoms. However, these are a functional disturbance and she is in no way abnormal nervously. The question is whether she has compulsive tendencies, and, if so, in what direction

the compulsions take her. There were no positive
indications of abnormal sexual preoccupations. It is
likely that the accused falls into the characterological
group simply called attention-seekers.

JUDGE: Show-offs?

PSYCHIATRIST: Precisely, milud. The wilful behaviour of
show-offs is clamorous and noisy. Their disabilities are
instability and flightiness. She is sexually abnormal in
that she lacks the capacity for human relationships.
Evidence is she frequently changes partners.

SCHNEIDER: I object. This evidence is inexact and
unscientific. If he had carried out his inquiries properly
he would know that Miss Munday has not changed
partners with me for a considerable time.

JUDGE: Please deny yourself your frivolity, Mr Schneider.
Proceed.

PSYCHIATRIST: This leads to her being unbalanced. Her
emotional life is unsteady and manic. She tends to he
superficially emotive. The make-up and ornamentation,
her hair-do, her bizarre clothes, all express a sense of
self-importance and reveal her deep sense of insecurity.

SCHNEIDER: Question. Your honour, your clothes are of
a bizarre nature which I would hesitate to emulate in the
King's Road. By that account, may I ask, what deep sense
of insecurity do they reveal in you? Milud, I sympathise.
I am too pressing. All this must be a trial for you. Shall
we adjourn?

JUDGE: I decide when to adjourn.

COUNSEL FOR THE PROSECUTION: To the case,
milud.

JUDGE: Thank you. 'Self-indictment of the Accused
Schneider.' I call Hans Schneider.

SCHNEIDER: Judicial motherfuckers, cretins of the Jury.

JUDGE: You must not insult the court.

SCHNEIDER: Then keep quiet. After workers and
prostitutes, the most universally despised person in
England is the student. This is because they are the most
exploited. The worker is fucked five days a week and it
only touches their hands. The prostitute is fucked six

days a week but only her cunt gets tired. Students are raped seven days a week – mind, body and soul. Eighty per cent of students come from income groups well above the working class, yet ninety per cent have less money than the lowest paid worker. Now the child is out in life, daddy won't provide: 'Your new family, Delia, darling, why that's your university. The state will pay.' We celebrate our dependence with all the anxiety of the infant at the breast: we shit in our pants. What don't we like? We don't like our illusions being destroyed. We thought universities were here to educate us. But a modern economic system demands the mass production of students who are not educated. Universities exist to render students incapable of thought. The best student is the one whose intelligence is most completely obliterated. Marks are awarded for conscientiously suppressing your ability. The university produces in the student all the appearance of knowledge without any of the reality. The 'educated' student is a bad joke. Your head is a can; now it's empty; now it's full. Print the brand name on the label and out you go to be consumed. That which appears is good, that which is good appears. Society is a spectacular organisation of appearances. Like everyone in society, students prefer the image to the thing itself. They love their slavery. The more chains heaped on them, the more they can fantasise. Reduced to perfect isolation, they only see one real alienation: their own. They become full-time happy consumers of themselves. Sanitised by Brut after-shave and Elizabeth Arden they disappear avidly up their own arse.

JUDGE: What is an arse?

COUNSEL FOR THE PROSECUTION: A kind of funeral vehicle, milud.

JUDGE: Thank you. I come to: 'Prophylactic Notes for the Self-Contraception of the Unborn Lucia Munday.' I call Miss Munday.

LUCIA: Rational and irrational authorities, ladies, gentlemen, students, comrades. I'm a nice student. A nice, mature student. I applied for enrolment, I read the conditions, I filled in the forms. I had a lover but I wrote down Miss because I'm not married. I said I was C of E, though I have no religion. I registered on Day One so I'd get my grant. I did not break into laughter when I sat in a row listening to lectures. Closing my eyes, I let the lecturers' words penetrate my mind. With assumed politeness I made myself obedient to the system. I collected the most fantastic facts about the American government's actions in Vietnam without in any way disturbing my neighbours. When I pointed out the university had business links in the development of weapons systems, the authorities complimented me on the objectivity of my research. If I was a little worried, they said, 'You should join one of the established parties and work to change things from within.' I was a little worried, so I joined the Labour Party. But when I demanded the end of the arms trade, unilateral nuclear disarmament, constituency control of Party policy and socialism in our time, they threw me out. Be realistic, they said, the world is a dirty place; we can only achieve what's possible. Why is it always impossible to demand the impossible? In Vietnam? In America? In Poland? With that lot in power, shouldn't I demand the air be made pure? Or do we have to stop breathing? I talked of genocide in Vietnam and they put up a notice, 'It is forbidden to step on the grass.' We were permitted to march, but immediately we changed the route, the police called out the riot squad. This gave me the idea that we first must destroy the lawn before they will take down their notices, we must change the route of the march before we can destroy the lies about Vietnam. My lover said, 'If they ever stop screwing my arse off, it's to come round and kick me in the balls.' His experience was always profoundly male.

JUDGE: What are balls?

COUNSEL FOR THE PROSECUTION: Spherical objects made of rubber or other material, used in the games of tennis and cricket, or for other purposes, milud.

JUDGE: Thank you. Mr Prosecutor.

COUNSEL FOR THE PROSECUTION: Well, Mr Schneider. Your self-indictment speaks for itself.

SCHNEIDER: Did you want to speak for it? Pity. I'd have let you.

COUNSEL FOR THE PROSECUTION: From what you said in it, you only made your unreliability that much more evident. What exactly was your intention in distributing that leaflet?

SCHNEIDER: Don't shout.

COUNSEL FOR THE PROSECUTION: I imagine you can't hear very well under all that hair.

SCHNEIDER: Now I can't understand you at all.

COUNSEL FOR THE PROSECUTION: Then I'll come a bit closer.

SCHNEIDER: Oh yes do! Come on!

JUDGE: Better not.

SCHNEIDER: Really? Why? Because I smell?

JUDGE: Yes, certainly. (*To the CLERK / STENOGRAPHER.*) Add 'Very much' after 'Yes, certainly'.

SCHNEIDER: I can't see it makes any difference.

COUNSEL FOR THE PROSECUTION: Just why did you distribute that leaflet?

SCHNEIDER: We were stimulated to moral indignation.

COUNSEL FOR THE PROSECUTION: When did this moral indignation strike you?

SCHNEIDER: Between the grapefruit juice and the bacon.

COUNSEL FOR THE PROSECUTION: I beg your pardon?

SCHNEIDER: It isn't something you read in the morning paper.

COUNSEL FOR THE PROSECUTION: What isn't? Incitement to assault?

SCHNEIDER: Oh no, you read that every day. No, I mean truth, a sense of justice, befriending the oppressed, that kind of thing.

COUNSEL FOR THE PROSECUTION: That kind of thing, eh? That includes attacks, doesn't it? Assaults. On individuals.

SCHNEIDER: Not any individual.

COUNSEL FOR THE PROSECUTION: Exactly. On individuals in positions of power! There's the monstrosity!

SCHNEIDER: Watch it! Don't speak ill of the judge.

COUNSEL FOR THE PROSECUTION: Miss Munday. Is he your lover?

LUCIA: Are you a virgin?

COUNSEL FOR THE PROSECUTION: Why did you write the leaflet?

LUCIA: We both wrote it. He used his right hand, I used my left.

COUNSEL FOR THE PROSECUTION: And what happens if someone gets the idea?

LUCIA: Marvellous.

COUNSEL FOR THE PROSECUTION: And assaults such a person?

LUCIA: Yes!

SCHNEIDER: Bravo!

COUNSEL FOR THE PROSECUTION: A banker.

LUCIA: Yes, yes.

COUNSEL FOR THE PROSECUTION: A financier.

SCHNEIDER: That's right.

COUNSEL FOR THE PROSECUTION: An MP.

LUCIA: Sure.

COUNSEL FOR THE PROSECUTION: A lord or an earl.

LUCIA: That's great.

SCHNEIDER: He's got the idea, judge.

COUNSEL FOR THE PROSECUTION: Or a general.

SCHNEIDER: That would be for real.

COUNSEL FOR THE PROSECUTION: Even the Queen.

SCHNEIDER: It has been done.

COUNSEL FOR THE PROSECUTION: That's incitement.

SCHNEIDER: Go on, you're very good.

COUNSEL FOR THE PROSECUTION: Incitement to assault.

SCHNEIDER: Ass-ault.

JUDGE: That's more like war, and I can tell you, we older people have experienced war.

SCHNEIDER: But you've forgotten. It's all idiocy.

COUNSEL FOR THE PROSECUTION: So you maintain the leaflet had no serious intent? It was all a joke.

SCHNEIDER: 'Joke' isn't the right word. Haven't you any trouble with your orgasms?

JUDGE: Counsel for the Defence.

COUNSEL FOR THE DEFENCE: In view of the report of the psychiatrist, as also of the self-indictments of the accused and their behaviour in court, it seems to me that what the two defendants are here accused of is theatre. One cannot say that we may deal with the expressive forms of modern art and literature in this way. Political satire, happenings and performance art or whatever they call it, can't be said to belong to the realm of the dangerous. When have you seen a gang of poseurs like these have any measurable effect at all on the real world? They create a spectacle and call it class war! The idea is preposterous. They should go home and mummy will change their nappies for them. My impression is there is no case to answer and I ask for the accused to be acquitted.

JUDGE: I direct the Jury there is no case.

(*As LUCIA and SCHNEIDER leave the court they are jostled by camera-happy press photographers snapping their pictures, while a TV cameraman gets his shots too.*)

7: Pillow Talk: Long Live Difference!

LUCIA and SCHNEIDER.

LUCIA: Why did I take second place?

SCHNEIDER: I wasn't aware of it.

LUCIA: I was much the lesser of the two. You made the judge a real idiot.

SCHNEIDER: He made himself that. You shouldn't see things in those terms. We ought to talk about our mutual experiences.

LUCIA: Mutual? You can talk like that because you have a bigger personality than me

SCHNEIDER: Not bigger. Different.

LUCIA: You don't know. The oppressed always know when they're oppressed.

SCHNEIDER: You cast me in the role of oppressor.

LUCIA: No. I'm just aware of the differences between us.

SCHNEIDER: And I'm aware of the shared experience. You don't deny we have that?

LUCIA: Oh we share what can be shared.

SCHNEIDER: You're talking like a riddle.

LUCIA: We share the same experience but experience it differently.

SCHNEIDER: Of course. There are contradictions in our unity.

LUCIA: There is unity in our contradictions.

SCHNEIDER: That's the same thing.

LUCIA: I don't think so.

SCHNEIDER: Just a different emphasis.

LUCIA: A different emphasis? Is that all? Doesn't the earth spin on that difference?

DIALOGUE ON ACTING

I'm an actress called Lucia Munday.

SCHNEIDER: You were an actress. You're not acting now.

LUCIA: 'You're not acting now.' Does that mean I've given up acting or I'm not acting just at this moment?

SCHNEIDER: You quit acting, Lucia.

LUCIA: When was that?

SCHNEIDER: A year ago. Two years.

LUCIA: I don't remember. I don't think I quit acting. You quit.

SCHNEIDER: I was never an actor. I just did a few parts. It was never my life.

LUCIA: My life was acting, was it?

SCHNEIDER: You know it was. For a while. It took you over.

LUCIA: It took me over. But now I'm clear of it.

SCHNEIDER: Yeah, you're not acting now.

LUCIA: Not at this moment?

SCHNEIDER: Not anytime.

LUCIA: It isn't my life?

SCHNEIDER: No, your life is fighting, liberation, the class war.

LUCIA: And not acting it? (*To audience.*) I was in this cage. The door was wide open but I couldn't escape. I stood in the middle of the cage, with a friend of mine, trying to think why I might want to escape. But I couldn't think of a reason. There was nothing I wanted outside. There was the same stale air out there. The same darkness. I stood there, feeling this urge, but unable to move. It was something important. No, I was acting as if it was something important. Acting as if something was happening, something significant was being played out. And I'd got used to it. It had become a habit. Suddenly I heard a laugh. It was my friend. I said to her, 'My love, we have nothing in common except the illusion of being together.' I expected her to laugh again but when I looked she wasn't there.

8: 'Let A Hundred Flowers Bloom!'

January 1969. Essex University Revolutionary Festival. STUDENTS. Genuine red banners. Jean-Luc GODARD.

STUDENT: Comrades. Monsieur Godard has come...
GODARD: Comrade Godard.
STUDENT: Thank you, comrade. Comrade Godard has flown in from Liberation Films Ltd of Paris specially to attend our Revolutionary Festival. Warm thanks to you, comrade.
(*Applauds. Others applaud. GODARD bows.*)
You have asked us, the Revolutionary Festival Street Theatre Group, to perform a typical revolutionary playlet for you to film. So you can destroy it by your editing. Fantastic! We reject the society of the spectacle!
GODARD: Shall I remove my glasses? (*Laughter.*)
STUDENT: Comrade Godard, we have chosen for you for this exemplary event a disgusting piece of crass bourgeois sensationalism –
(*GODARD licks his lips or makes similar consumerist noises.*)
– not unlike your own work.
GODARD: (*Presents his arse.*) Beat me.

STUDENT: It's called 'Dis'. Not 'Dat' but 'Dis'. There are
    five characters. (*Introduces the actors.*) Dis, a boy of five.
    Let, Dis's brother, aged four.
    (*Played by a BLACK STUDENT.*)
    Their Mother. Ferdinand, their Father.
    (*Played by SCHNEIDER.*)
    Girl, aged three.
    (*Played by LUCIA.*)
GODARD: (*Calls.*) Camera!
    (*CAMERAMAN sets up camera.*)
    I just crank up my English vice a little. (*Presents his arse
    to the lens while a minion whips it.*) Enough.
STUDENT: Are we ready?
GODARD: (*Eye to the camera.*) Dziga Vertov! Roll!
STUDENT: (*Announces.*) Dis, or the Thousand and One
    Days of the Nuclear Family.

DIS

(*A playroom. Toys, mobiles, high chair, LET and DIS.*)
DIS: Angle between spaces.
LET: Corroborate.
DIS: Angle between spaces.
LET: Magnitude.
DIS: War. Space.
LET: Minitude.
DIS: War.
LET: Corroborate.
DIS: War.
    (*Enter MOTHER with a slice of bread.*)
MOTHER: Butter.
DIS: Don't.
MOTHER: I wan' butter.
DIS: Don't.
MOTHER: I wan' butter.
DIS: You'll make me cross.
MOTHER: Mama hungry.
DIS: I'll give you a good spanking.
    (*MOTHER cries.*)

There, there. Don't take on.

(*MOTHER cries.*)

Hushaby.

(*MOTHER cries. DIS calls.*)

Ferdinand.

(*MOTHER cries. DIS calls.*)

Ferdinand.

(*Enter their father FERDINAND on all fours in a dog's skin. He sniffs around, growling and gruffing. To FERDINAND.*)

Savage, Ferdie.

(*MOTHER cries.*)

LET: Give her some, Dis, don't tease her.

(*MOTHER stops crying. FERDINAND growls loudly.*)

DIS: Evangelical.

LET: Turpitude.

DIS: Space.

LET: Fathom.

DIS: Evangelical.

LET: Fathom.

DIS: War.

LET: Crux.

DIS: Pursuit.

(*LET gives MOTHER some butter. DIS snatches it from her. MOTHER cries, louder.*)

FERDINAND: Snit. Gogle. Lawl.

DIS: How dare you speak till you're spoken to.

(*FERDINAND growls. MOTHER tries to snatch the butter.*)

Stop it, you little devil.

(*MOTHER cries louder still and throws the bread to the ground. DIS treads on it.*)

So much for that, damn you. I rue the day you were born.

(*MOTHER sulks.*)

FERDINAND: Jacknapingskl.

(*DIS kicks FERDINAND.*)

DIS: Take off that filthy old skin. You are being tiresome today.

(*Pulls at the dog's skin. FERDINAND backs and barks.*)

Ferdie! D'you hear what I say? Off with it.

(*He holds on to the skin and as FERDINAND pulls back, it peels off. Underneath, FERDINAND is naked.*)

LET: What a stench. Didn't you wash this morning?

FERDINAND: No.

LET: Why not?

FERDINAND: Mama took the soap away.

LET: Did you take the soap away from Ferdie?

MOTHER: He's a bastard.

LET: Don't say things like that. Jesus wouldn't like it. He'd say: 'You shouldn't use wicked words like that.' Don't you love Jesus?

FERDINAND: No.

LET: You're just being difficult today. I'll send you to bed.

(*MOTHER cries, FERDINAND growls.*)

DIS: What is it now?

FERDINAND: Col'-col'.

DIS: Go and get dressed then.

FERDINAND: Mama took my clothes away.

DIS: Did you take his clothes away?

MOTHER: I wan' bread.

DIS: Where're Ferdie's clothes?

MOTHER: I wan' puppy.

DIS: Ferdinand.

FERDINAND: I'm col'.

(*MOTHER screams and throws herself on the floor where she convulses.*)

LET: Negritude.

DIS: Philosophiser.

LET: Sanctity.

DIS: Angle between spaces.

LET: Contemplate.

DIS: Angle war space war.

LET: Between.

DIS: Space war angle war.

LET: Between.

(*LET throws a blanket over MOTHER. He whips it off. He lifts a little naked girl from between MOTHER's legs.*)

DIS: Girl.

LET: Girl. Dead.

(He puts it down on the floor FERDINAND rushes up, still on all fours, and licks it, panting and puffing.)

DIS: Down, Ferdie.

(FERDINAND licks the body more enthusiastically.)

Stop it, I tell you.

(LET pushes FERDINAND away and prods the body with his foot.)

LET: Dead.

DIS: It's three.

LET: Born three.

MOTHER: Too big girlie boyso.

DIS: Starch.

LET: Supreme.

DIS: War luck.

LET: Space.

DIS: War angle.

FERDINAND: Papa go-go lick-lick girlie.

(LET restrains him.)

MOTHER: I wan' bread.

DIS: Get up.

MOTHER: Mama col'-col'.

LET: She's lost blood.

MOTHER: I wan' clothes.

FERDINAND: You got clothes.

(LET tosses MOTHER the dog's skin. She pulls it over her head like a blanket. FERDINAND, barking, rushes at her and tears it off her: he savages her. As her screams and his growls and barks intensify.)

DIS: Good dog, Ferdie. Well done. Good dog.

LET: Corroborate magnitude minitude corroborate.

DIS: Angle between spaces angle between spaces war space war war.

LET: *(Shouting.)* Corroborate magnitude minitude corroborate.

DIS: *(Shouting.)* Angle between spaces angle between spaces war space war war.

(The dead GIRL gets up and walks out.)

(Shouting.) Girl.

(*Silence of all. DIS runs out. He re-enters, dragging the GIRL.*)

LET: You're dead.

DIS: It's three.

LET: Born dead.

DIS: Born three. (*Pause. To the GIRL.*) Well?

(*Silence. The GIRL begins to sob.*)

GODARD: (*Applauds.*) Magnifique! The kino-eye is the kino-revolution. Let us agree again: the ear to the door, the eye to the peep-hole. The ear, the eye and the arse; c'est le cinéma! Have you the script?

(*BLACK STUDENT hands him some papers.*)

Is dis the script? (*Laughs.*) How much do you want for it? Camera!

(*The camera turns. Pulls out wallet like a gun.*)

Ah you see, I've come well armed! How much? Ten thousand francs?

STUDENT: Well Monsieur Godard...

GODARD: Done! (*Gives STUDENT the money, takes the papers. Glances at the title.*) Merde! (*Reads.*) 'Essex Situationists. Manifesto 81. Against the Society of the Spectacle. We demand: Smash all cameras!' (*To CAMERAMAN.*) Cut! (*To STUDENT.*) This is not 'Dis'!

(*STUDENTS laugh. To audience.*)

'My friendly warning:

Don't bury your heads like ostriches.

Raise your eyes,

Look around –

There!

Seen by me and by every child's eye:

Insides falling out.

Intestines of experience

Out of the belly of cinemaphotography

slashed

By the reef of the revolution,

there they drag,

leaving a bloody trace on the ground,

shuddering from terror and repulsion.'

9: Pillow Talk: Let There Be Light!

January 1969. LUCIA places a gun under their pillow.

SCHNEIDER: Strike at the real. (*Silence.*)
LUCIA: Illusions can't strike.
    (*Silence. Speaks to audience.*)
    If you want to know me
    study a log of white wood.
    Look at it closely –
    see the stripped bark,
    see the white limbs
    carved and worked.
    Hands carved it,
    rough hands chiseled it,
    a mind like a poet's worked it –
    that's what I am:
    eyes gouged out,
    mouth torn open,
    that's what I am –
    body turned,
    flesh scoured,
    (*Sings.*) that's what I am.
    (*Silence.*)
SCHNEIDER: What kind of a song was that?
LUCIA: A poem to beauty.
SCHNEIDER: You should sing songs.
LUCIA: I'm not a good singer.
SCHNEIDER: Songs are good to resist with. Specially sad ones. About suffering. What's a song? A song is comradeship. It shows others are suffering too. It's a provocation. It shows resistance is possible.
LUCIA: (*Laughs.*) I must learn singing.
SCHNEIDER: You've got a beautiful voice but it needs technique.
LUCIA: Oh to be trained in singing and shooting! Then I'd be really beautiful.
SCHNEIDER: Then you'll resist.
LUCIA: Full of light. Resist with light. What creates light?
SCHNEIDER: The sun.

LUCIA: The sun is on fire.

SCHNEIDER: I learnt to sing under the Nazis. All the communist workers' songs. My mother taught me. But she also said, 'Whatever you do, don't sing them. Get that into your head.' And she told me why. So I only sang them at home. At home in the morning between five and seven. At five my mother went to work in the ammunition factory. At seven my aunt came to look after me for the day. So for two hours I lay in bed alone. I was frightened, so I sang. (*Sings.*)

Lots of people will make sure that
socialism triumphs here –
now! Today and not tomorrow!
Don't keep waiting for the good times...

LUCIA: Teach me to sing.

SCHNEIDER: I'm not your mother.

(*Pause.*)

LUCIA: Let there be light!

(*Pause.*)

SCHNEIDER: If you do it, I'll leave you.

(*LUCIA sets fire to the Imperial War Museum. The stage is consumed by flames. The auditorium does not escape, either.*)

10: On The Run

Summer 1969. LUCIA addresses the workers.

LUCIA: Comrade workers, it appears you have stopped working. If you've gone on strike, it's because you have demands to make. Workers' demands are just demands. I set fire to the Imperial War Museum. Comrades, that Museum was full of trophies of war, paintings of battles, planes, tanks, guns. All of it singing the praises of war. What has war done for us, comrades? We are the people it slaughters. We are the people they lead to our deaths. Who leads us? Comrades, you want a rise. Who from? From the bosses? Do you go down on your knees to them? 'Please sir, give me another five quid?' They are planning to kill you. With their missiles and bombs,

they're going to vaporise you, comrades, they're going to
melt you down, turn you into thin air – and you plead
with them for five pounds? For five bits of paper with the
Queen's head on, you'll give them your lives?
Comrades, the peasants killed by napalm in the
American war in Vietnam, the thirty million workers
killed in Europe in the world war did not expect to die
for a generation who'd say, 'I want to forget.' Forget the
murderers? Forget we're living in a society of
murderers? Forget that to combat them, we are forced to
kill them? Or are you lemmings? Is that it? Is it my
moral duty to take away the sea? (*In a low voice.*)
Comrades, can you give me a room for tonight?

11: Unit Three Derails A Weapons Train

*Winter 1969. A tight hole, front or back, upper storey or basement
flat. The Aldershot Brigade. A group meeting. There are six in the
group: LUCIA, RUTH, CLAUDIA (an Italian), WINSTON (a
West Indian), LESZEK and PAUL.*

RUTH: (*To LUCIA.*) Sheila!
  (*LUCIA looks startled. They embrace.*)
LUCIA: Thanks for the money, Ruth. I was starving.
RUTH: That's okay. I'm Stella.
PAUL: Are you sisters?
RUTH: You're not to know. (*To LUCIA.*) Don't take any
  notice. (*To LESZEK.*) We're over here, Les.
LUCIA: When's the meeting, Stella?
RUTH: Now! Come on, sit near me.
  (*The six take their places.*)
CLAUDIA: This is the big day, yeah?
LESZEK: Better be.
WINSTON: I'll take look-out, okay?
LESZEK: Okay.
RUTH: Comrades, the active core has met in a confined
  space. Rather like this. Which led to some overheating.
  And a bit of unnecessary fission. Anyway, Les will
  deliver our report. It's to help us decide our next action.

175

It's based on the analysis we've already agreed: when
conditions will be ripe for armed struggle, it will be too
late to prepare for it. But equally, remember, we've
rejected spontaneism. We have our tactics. We're
unfolding a distinct and rigorous strategy. Our report
makes that clear.
WINSTON: It better have.
RUTH: Les.

STATE OF THE WORLD MESSAGE:
A COLLECTIVE MONOLOGUE

LESZEK: (*Reads.*) 'If we are slowly breaking the grip of the
oppressive state machine, it is because we have our eyes
on the majority of the people, on their suffering and
liberation. For centuries, visionaries have promised
utopia and built prisons. We're not interested in utopia.
We won't force people to be more revolutionary than a
consciousness of their own oppression will force them to
be. It's more important to continue the revolution than
to 'win' it. We don't seek through a majority to bring
about a revolution. We use revolutionary tactics to bring
about a majority. Our example is our deeds; by our acts
let us be judged. It is on this general basis that we
organise our actions.
(*The BRIGADE break out of the confined space, line up and
do physical training exercises.*)
'But our tactics also have their context in a larger
strategy. To organise the urban guerrilla means to take
the offensive in anti-imperialist struggle. Our actions
create a link between legal and illegal struggle, between
political and armed struggle, between national and
international struggle, between Europe and the Third
World; between the tactical and strategic dimensions of
the international communist movement. Our comrades
are in Berlin, in Warsaw, in Peking, in Angola, in
Mozambique, in Nicaragua. They are underground, too.
We reply to their actions with our own but we're not the
same as them, they are not the same as us. We are
produced by the state of Britain. Take us away and the

conditions which produced us would produce others like us. We're always necessary, especially when we're least wanted.

(*As the Report continues the other members of the Brigade disperse into action, enacting in detail and with precision the mission they will choose at the end of the Report – Unit Three derails an atomic-weapons train.*)

'What are the political features of this larger strategic context? First, the struggle in the Third World. One after another the countries of the Third World are completing their liberation. Their post-war victories against the old European imperial powers have been followed by a series of victories against US imperialism. This marks the end of the post-war phase of world domination by the West. The United States is no longer the leading world power. Secondly, the October Revolution in Russia determined the way capitalism was to develop in the West. By its existence as an alternative state system, the Soviet Union forced capitalism into the open, forced it to shove its ideology into the minds of the masses, making them slaves not only with their hands but in their hearts and minds, creating in the West a supine class far more deeply subjugated than before they got the vote, their relative prosperity compared with the starving in the Third World being bought at the cost of their dignity and solidarity. The line between the United States and the Soviet Union is a wound which scars the face of the earth and distorts the features of its peoples. That wound runs down the middle of Europe. The first inroad into capitalist relationships has made brothers enemies of brothers, isolated sister from sister. We cannot make further inroads if our actions here in England are not carried out in brotherhood and sisterhood with workers in the Soviet Union, in the United States, across the divide. We emphatically do not recognise any iron curtain separating us from our comrades. The bonds we feel as workers with workers in those countries are stronger than the fear we have of the capitalists and their national boundaries, their armies which patrol them and the forces of law and order which keep us inside them. This monstrous fraud of separation, this deception perpetrated on the peoples of the world is backed by a grotesque and obscene stock-pile of weapons of destruction. The manufacture and deployment of these weapons determine our economy and control the direction of the nation's politics and social life. The civil economy becomes the military economy, and those who reject that as immoral are branded 'the enemy within'. Dissent becomes 'disloyalty to democracy' and those who still continue to resist are forced to give up any hope of reasoning with those responsible, leaving them no alternative but the exile of illegality. The choices open to us are those they dictated to us. We've learned a truth that resistance workers everywhere learn when they face up to their oppression: in struggle, illegality is the only liberated area.

'The active core makes the following proposals:

Unit One: bomb RSG number 85,

Unit Two: bomb US air-base number 19,

Unit Three: atomic-weapons train 251, derail at point B.

Proposal accepted; Unit Three, derail train 251.'

(*Only the voice has remained. Unit Three, having prepared the derailment, awaits the outcome. The cyclorama depicts the railway track; on the sound system, the train approaches, not very fast – a low drone of the diesel engine, a lonely clanking of couplings. As the engine speeds up – a huge scraping. wrenching and tearing as the locomotive leaves the rails. The Brigade disperses silently.*)

12: Shoot-out At Barracks Street

Spring 1970. The Aldershot Brigade is in an inside room on an upper storey, occupying positions from which they can fire down into the street (out the back of the stage). They are tense, alert; their weapons are ready trained on the street; waiting.

TRADITIONS

CLAUDIA: In a hut he lay wounded. In the reeds. Wounded
in the leg. Couldn't run, couldn't walk. He lay in the
straw. The hut was used by hunters; they came shooting
duck. It was midsummer. Mosquitoes. Flies. His leg was
raw, open. He had no ammunition left. He'd chucked his
gun in the water. Crawled to the hut through the marsh.
A peasant woman found him. She thought my father had
lain there about four days before he died.

LESZEK: My mother blew up trains. On the line from
Warsaw to Cracow. Once her group were holding a
meeting in a peasant's house, in the only room, no way
to escape, when the fascists arrived in the village. Some
quisling had tipped them off. There was a loud noise
outside. My mother broke the top off a glass phial she
was carrying. The peasant came in and said, 'It's only the
women at the river beating their washing.' The others in
the group grabbed my mother and pumped her stomach.
She was ill for three weeks but she lived. The poison
destroyed her digestion. She could never take meat
again, just soft eggs and milk. I was in her womb at the
time.

RUTH: You know nothing, Leszek.

LESZEK: I do. From the inside.

RUTH: In the camps it was wise to renounce even your own
body. Renounce everything. Even people who were close
to you were your enemies. Redeem your soul and you'd
save your body. I believe that. Only the spirit saves. The
spirit supports the body. Poverty and prison give
wisdom. For stupid people, look in governments. For
intelligent people, look in prisons. Survive! Look! Our
prison isn't in here. It's the sky outside!

LESZEK: Make love, make love!

RUTH: With a bullet in your vibrator.

WINSTON: It's awful lonely,
lonely,
like screaming,
screaming in a dark alley,

a scream loud and clear
none can hear
echoing
for you, for you –
shouting a pain, screaming a prayer. (*Song ends.*)
I talk to myself too much.

PAUL: I have a sister. In the county set. Married to a
financier. In the jet set. Big house. In the gin-and-tonic
belt. Leatherhead, Camberley, somewhere. Dad's a
military man, a farmer in Rhodesia, fought in Greece.
Retired to the home country. Dozens of medals. True
blue. I'm his failure.

(*From high behind the audience comes heavy fire. SAS MEN
rush the Brigade from the rear, moving through the auditorium.
A TV CAMERA CREW accompanies them, with REPORTER.
LESZEK and CLAUDIA are killed. WINSTON offers to
give himself up but they shoot him dead. They overpower
LUCIA, RUTH (who is wounded) and PAUL and hustle
them off.*)

FIRST SAS: Laughable gits!

SECOND SAS: Couldn't organise a piss-up.

FIRST SAS: 'Alf of 'em bloody foreigners.

SECOND SAS: Black shit an' all.

THIRD SAS: Fuckin' bastards. (*Turns over a corpse.*) 'Ere's
the bloody Iti.

FOURTH SAS: 'Ave fun, eh?

FIRST SAS: Get medals for this.

SECOND SAS: The nation's grateful.

THIRD SAS: Services to the EEC.

SECOND SAS: Go anywhere, do anythin'.

THIRD SAS: Britain does 'er bit.

FIRST SAS: We're all patriots now.

SECOND SAS: Calls for a toast.

THIRD SAS: Why not? Fuckin' thirsty.

FOURTH SAS: Try 'er.

THIRD SAS: Good idea.

(*They dip their fingers in CLAUDIA's blood.*)

FOURTH SAS: Bloody cunt juice.

(*They hold out their fingers.*)

THIRD SAS: To the European Community!
ALL: To the European Community!
  (*They touch fingers. They taste their finger tips.*)

13: Lucia In Prison

A table, with two chairs on opposite sides. A WOMAN WARDER, A MAN WARDER, standing by, watching.

LUCIA: (*To audience.*) I dreamed I was this other person. I
  was sitting in a row. With a lot of other people. Watching
  a woman open a door. She stood by the wall, swinging
  the door on its hinges, thinking. She never quite shut it,
  just stopped it short and pulled it back. Easily.
  Rhythmically. She did this for a long time; she never
  looked round the cell, which was bare and white. No
  window, just a very bright light. Terribly white. She
  seemed to be completely absorbed in the movement of
  the door, opening it and shutting it, absolutely wrapped
  up in it. I thought, 'I'm watching her beauty, I'm
  watching her wisdom, I'm watching her skill.'
  (*Enter SCHNEIDER. They sit at the table, opposite each
  other.*)

DIATRIBE ON NON-VIOLENCE

SCHNEIDER: I'm sorry they got you.
LUCIA: Thanks. (*Pause.*) How's Christine?
SCHNEIDER: She has a cold. I got a neighbour to look
  after her. (*Pause.*) She's walking now.
LUCIA: Is she?
  (*Pause.*)
SCHNEIDER: The swine.
LUCIA: Who?
SCHNEIDER: They didn't let you have her.
LUCIA: I wouldn't have agreed to have her.
SCHNEIDER: Yes you would.
LUCIA: You're perfectly capable of bringing her up.
  (*Pause.*)

SCHNEIDER: I'm sorry I haven't come before.

LUCIA: I had your letter. (*Pause.*) I understand. You hate all that.

SCHNEIDER: There are a lot of things wrong. A lot has to be done.

LUCIA: But – so far and no further!

SCHNEIDER: If it leads to that, yes.

LUCIA: Leads to what?

SCHNEIDER: People died.

LUCIA: Is that what your paper says?

SCHNEIDER: I'm not responsible for what my editor writes.

LUCIA: No. Because you have a nice fat cheque at the end of the month.

SCHNEIDER: It's not that.

LUCIA: What is it then? Don't you like killing?

SCHNEIDER: What?

LUCIA: Would you never kill?

SCHNEIDER: Human life has an absolute value.

LUCIA: Does it? But it feels so good!

SCHNEIDER: Not to the person killed.

LUCIA: They don't feel anything. I think they die for the living.

SCHNEIDER: You're twisted.

LUCIA: You sound like one of your editorials. (*Pause.*) What if you came face to face with a tiger in the jungle?

SCHNEIDER: It doesn't happen very often.

LUCIA: But if it did.

SCHNEIDER: I'd do the best I can.

LUCIA: You'd kill it as best you could.

SCHNEIDER: The whole world is fucked up.

LUCIA: What are you going to do? Complain to the manufacturer?

SCHNEIDER: You think it was necessary? To use guns?

LUCIA: No. But it happened.

SCHNEIDER: It was gratuitous. You had the choice.

LUCIA: You actually believe that! You do, don't you! You're not being hypocritical. You actually believe in your own deceit. You're almost English. You want to die slowly, in ignorance, like a slave.

SCHNEIDER: It doesn't mean passivity. Non-violence means strikes, sabotage. The weapons train was terrific.

LUCIA: Thanks.

SCHNEIDER: You see? It means cunning, intellect, treason.

LUCIA: Art? Poetry? Cunt?

SCHNEIDER: You're crazy.

LUCIA Did you come here to insult me?

SCHNEIDER: Lucia! (*Pause.*) Is this all there is? (*Pause.*) We knew each other better than that. Why are you so hostile? I'm not your enemy.

LUCIA: Hostile! You're just like them. You provoke a reaction and then you accuse the protestor of hostility.

SCHNEIDER: Well you *are* crazy if you think I'm in their keep.

LUCIA: It's simple. I'm against people who cause violence. I'm not against people who resist violence.

SCHNEIDER: But that'll never end. You're locked together. It'll go on and on.

LUCIA: Yes, on and on. My mother worked on the line. In a weapons factory. Packing high explosives.

SCHNEIDER: You never knew your mother.

LUCIA: Are you accusing me of lying?

SCHNEIDER: You told me. You never even knew what she was like.

LUCIA: You're right.

SCHNEIDER: Your foster-mother picked you up out of the rubble.

LUCIA: (*Lost.*) Huh! Yes. I was born dead. (*Recovers.*) Yeah. She told me. Told me who I was. Mother. Fucker.

SCHNEIDER: You're disgusting.

LUCIA: Your blood is up! Throbs in your veins.

SCHNEIDER: You're crazy!

LUCIA: Poor Hans, you've got a hard-on.

RIPOSTE ON THE LOVE OF THE BLOOD RUSH

SCHNEIDER: You're mad!

LUCIA: (*With longing.*) No!

SCHNEIDER: Lucia!

LUCIA: I tell you, it's simple, Hans. Your head feels like a great sun. Your whole body is flooded with blood, warm, rushing. It's as if you're bathing in it, deep, thick. You let it wash over your legs, your arms, your shoulders, your face. You can taste its salt. Haven't you felt that? Don't deny it. Don't you feel it every time?

SCHNEIDER: I've never killed.

(*LUCIA laughs deeply. Pause.*)

LUCIA: I always thought you were so clever. I see what an idiot I was. I wasn't talking about killing. Bad luck. You'd better find someone else. Anyway, dirty weekends here aren't very nice. The beds don't have any springs and you don't get much privacy. Even if you like being watched, it's not the best audience. You'd better go. (*Embraces him.*) My enemy is the person who tells me who my enemy is.

(*SCHNEIDER goes.*)

(*To audience.*) Sometimes, there's a huge sky and I'm looking up. This pilot has come down in flames. He's a mass of flesh and bones but then I see his face. Very young, about seventeen. I'm smiling at him and stroking his face.

(*Enter RUTH as LUCIA's 'sister'. She embraces LUCIA. They sit at the table, opposite each other.*)

LUCIA: I'm sorry.

RUTH: What for?

LUCIA: I flared up at you last time.

RUTH: I know.

LUCIA: I've been waiting to tell you.

RUTH: It doesn't matter. (*Pause.*) I got you a sweater. (*Pushes a woollen sweater across the table.*) Do you like it?

LUCIA: It's lovely.

RUTH: I tried it on. It should fit.

LUCIA: Nice and thick.

RUTH: Did they put the heating on?

LUCIA: No.

RUTH: I told them they're sadistic.

LUCIA: Is that all?

RUTH: They're breaking the regulations.

LUCIA: They will if they want to. It doesn't matter.

RUTH: It does matter. (*Pause.*) Are you all right?

LUCIA: Yeah, I'm all right. (*Pause.*) The screw on my wing says, 'You got a lovely sister.'

RUTH: Aren't you lucky!

LUCIA: If only they knew!
   (*They laugh. Pause.*)

RUTH: You been dreaming.

LUCIA: Yeah.

RUTH: Bags under your eyes. Must've been dreaming about me.

LUCIA: Yeah!

RUTH: Yeah?

LUCIA: I was!

RUTH: Were you?
   (*Pause.*)

LUCIA Hans came to see me. At last.

RUTH: Did he?

LUCIA: That was the bad dream.
   (*They laugh. Pause.*)

RUTH: Do you need anything then?

LUCIA: No, they give you everything here. A tissue to cry on. One tampax every month. A pistol to shoot yourself with.
   (*They laugh.*)
   And you. Are you better now?

RUTH: Yeah.

LUCIA: Quite recovered?

RUTH: 'Course I have. Strong as an 'orse.

LUCIA: Renounced your body, have you?

RUTH: Yeah.

LUCIA: Redeemed your soul?

RUTH: I've renounced everything.

LUCIA: You certainly carry out your own instructions.

MAN WARDER: Time's up.

SLEEPERS' SONG

LUCIA: (*At table, to audience, sings.*)
    When they come
    when they come
    you will be sleeping
    but the sleeper will wake –
LUCIA / RUTH: I'll show them the way.
RUTH: When they come
    when they come
    you may be caught napping
    but I'll give them a reception –
RUTH / LUCIA: I'll see they go home.
LUCIA: When they come
    when they come
    you'll look one way
    but I'll look the other –
LUCIA / RUTH: I'll take them along.
    When they come
    when they come
    I don't know about you
    but I'll be ready and waiting
    to open the door
    to open the door.
RUTH: So you don't want anything?
    (*RUTH gets up to go. In one action RUTH takes a gun from
    her coat and covers the MAN WARDER while LUCIA takes
    a gun from the sweater RUTH brought and covers the
    WOMAN WARDER, as they go off.*)

14: The Archbishop Exorcises Lucia

*Enter ARCHBISHOP OF CANTERBURY, with ATTENDANT
carrying water, in a vessel, salt and a piece of sackcloth.*

ARCHIBISHOP: (*To the salt.*) Every evil spirit depart from
    this salt. Lord, bless this salt. (*To the water.*) Every evil
    spirit depart from this water. Lord, bless this water.
    (*The ATTENDANT mixes the salt and water.*)

Almighty Father, look with mercy on this creature of salt
and water, sanctify it with your loving kindness.
Wherever it shall be sprinkled with the invocation of
your holy Name may the attacks of evil spirits be
repelled.

(*Enter TWO STRONG MEN with LUCIA. She has
wandered. She is listless. The MEN remove her shoes and
outer clothing. The ATTENDANT lays out the sackcloth on
the ground. The STRONG MEN stand LUCIA before the
ARCHBISHOP.*)

Face the west.

(*The STRONG MEN face LUCIA to the west.*)

Lower your eyes.

(*LUCIA does so.*)

ALL FOUR MEN: Lead us not into temptation but deliver
us from evil. Amen.

ARCHBISHOP: In the beginning was the Word, and the
Word was with God, and the Word was God.

(*A moment of silent prayer; then he begins the exorcism.*)
I command you, every evil spirit, in the Name of God the
Father Almighty, in the Name of Jesus Christ his only
Son, and in the Name of the Holy Spirit, that, harming no-
one, you depart from this creature of God, and return to
the place appointed you, there to remain for ever.

(*ARCHBISHOP exhales deeply. He sprinkles LUCIA with
the holy water. She struggles, shrieks, whines and barks. She
tries to escape; the STRONG MEN drag her back.*)
Bind her!

(*The STRONG MEN drag LUCIA to a chair. She struggles,
resisting them with power, screaming. They hold her down
and bind her. The ARCHBISHOP blows on her, making the
sign of the cross on her forehead. They subdue her somewhat.*)
Is she cold?

FIRST STRONG MAN: (*Feels LUCIA's forehead.*) Cold as a
dog's nose, Archbishop.

(*ARCHBISHOP approaches LUCIA again. She kicks him
away.*)

LUCIA: Don't you dare come a step forward.

(*She sprawls on the chair, legs apart. She speaks with another's
voice.*)

ARCHBISHOP: I put you on oath by the living God to tell me if you are the Christ.

LUCIA: The Lord be fucked.

ARCHBISHOP: All things in heaven and earth, everything visible and invisible, thrones, dominions, sovereignties, powers, all were created through Him and for Him. Demons, tremble in fear before Him. Unclean spirits, obey Him.

LUCIA: Whip her. She loves Him. Whip her arse.

ARCHBISHOP: Go forth, thou deceiver, persecutor of the innocent. Give place, thou wicked one, give place, thou evil one, give place to Christ.

LUCIA: She sucks Him off.

(*ARCHBISHOP spits on LUCIA. She retches and convulses. The STRONG MEN hold her still.*)

Don't be afraid.

ARCHBISHOP: Rather you should not fear the power of the Lord. In the Name of Jesus. renounce your evil, find absolution in the Name of Jesus, seek liberation in surrender to the Lord.

LUCIA: You don't believe me.

ARCHBISHOP: Believe in me, saith the Lord, and the demons shall be cast out.

LUCIA: I want to kill Lucia.

ARCHBISHOP: Why?

(*LUCIA spits at him.*)

Answer me!

LUCIA: She wants to serve the Lord. You don't believe me, do you?

ARCHBISHOP: I don't believe in the devil.

LUCIA: Who licked his wife off last night?

ARCHBISHOP: (*Confused.*) What?

LUCIA: (*Sarcastically.*) You should believe in me. She says she loves him.

ARCHBISHOP: Loves who?

LUCIA: (*Angrily.*) You know who. (*Spits the words like a curse.*) Karl Marx. (*In her own voice.*) God and Devil – two sides of the same coin, Archbishop. As for us, your money's tainted. Lucia isn't Lucifer, and God can go to

the devil. We're going to mint a new currency. And it'll
pass between us in free exchange. No slaves. No
servitude.

(*The ARCHBISHOP sits on a stool and wipes his brow.*)

ARCHBISHOP: Christ be with me, Christ within me,
Christ behind me, Christ before me, Christ on my left
hand, Christ on my right hand, Christ below me, Christ
above me, Christ be with me. All beings bend the knee
at the Name of Jesus, every tongue acclaims Jesus Christ
as Lord. The devil is sent out by the blood of the Lamb.
No demon can pass the Blood line. Lord, fill the empty
vessel with the love of God. (*To himself.*) Do not rejoice
that the spirits submit to you. (*Falls asleep.*)

(*The STRONG MEN untie LUCIA. She gives them each a
CND badge, which they put on. She takes her shoes and
clothes.*)

LUCIA: (*To audience.*) One night the Archbishop prayed for
peace. He said war was a totally unacceptable means of
settling differences between nations, it belongs to the
past and should find no place on humanity's agenda for
the future. I wept and turned to him. He embraced me
and said, 'Totus tuus. I am all yours.' I woke up,
sweating.

15: Your Orders When It Comes To It

LUCIA and RUTH are making love.

RUTH: The President has approved a plan (*Kisses LUCIA on
the face.*) to defeat the Soviet Union and to do so at a cost
that would enable the United States to recover. (*Kisses
LUCIA.*) The State Department envisages a nuclear war
fought over a period of months (*Pauses.*) with selective
strikes against enemy military and command centres. It
aims to destroy Soviet political authority (*Kisses LUCIA.*)
and looks forward to the emergence of a post-war world
order compatible with Western values.

LUCIA: (*With love.*) In the event of a nuclear exchange, the
United States post office will suspend registered and
express mail. (*Pause.*) Those fleeing the disaster areas will

be given change of address cards. (*Pause.*) As a
concession in disaster areas, 'scenic view' picture
postcards will be accepted without stamps.
As I walk along the street
as blind as a bat
I think
I will never see the world
till I die.
As a blind man
I can't see one thing
in this lovely world
dark is a terrible thing
to live with.

YOUR ORDERS WHEN IT COMES TO IT

RUTH: At the slightest sign
    their war preparations are reaching a climax
    you should occupy the command centres
LUCIA: At the slightest sign
    their government is getting ready to press the button
    you should walk into Downing Street
RUTH: At the slightest sign
    their officials are about to go underground
    you should haul them out of their bunkers
LUCIA: At the slightest sign
    their generals are going to use their fire power
    you should disarm the generals
RUTH: At the slightest sign
    their councillors are finalising civil defence measures
    you should barricade the council chambers
LUCIA: At the slightest sign
    their messages are giving the go-ahead
    you should sabotage their secret communications
    network
RUTH: At the slightest sign
    their police are issuing orders to shoot those who protest
    you should disarm the police

LUCIA: At the slightest sign
   their bombers are lifting off
   you should destroy the bombers
RUTH: At the slightest sign
   they are targetting their missiles
   you should open fire on your target
LUCIA: At the slightest sign
   they are handing out rifles to annihilate you
   you should make sure you get to the armoury first.

Epilogue

1982. At a peace camp outside a US air-base in East Anglia. An empty space. Silence. LUCIA and SCHNEIDER enter. They examine the steel gates, the concrete posts, the wire fence topped with barbed wire, the 'Keep Out!' and 'USAF' notices in red lettering. They lie across the entrance to the base, head to head. Their mood is quiet as if this is pillow talk, a dream. They speak their lines with deliberation, spacing them with care.

LUCIA: I love you, Hans Schneider.
SCHNEIDER: We are all undesirables.
LUCIA: Think of your desires as realities.
SCHNEIDER: The more I revolt, the more I make love.
LUCIA: Prohibiting is forbidden.
SCHNEIDER: Power is on the run. Let it fall.
LUCIA: Imagination usurps power.
SCHNEIDER: Today I'm seeing the future.
LUCIA: Everyone has to breathe.
SCHNEIDER: No-one can say, 'Hang on, you can breathe later.'
LUCIA: We are not abnormal.
SCHNEIDER: The world is.
LUCIA: Don't change bosses. Change life.
SCHNEIDER: Revolutionise my prick.
LUCIA: He is violent when oppressed, he is gentle when he is free.
SCHNEIDER: When the last psychiatrist is hanged by the guts of the last bureaucrat, will we still have problems?

LUCIA: Be kind to be cruel.

SCHNEIDER: Forget everything you've been taught. Start dreaming.

LUCIA: Put a pig in your tank.

SCHNEIDER: If you can't feel angry, don't look.

LUCIA: Revolution stops immediately you have to be sacrificed to it.

SCHNEIDER: Our crime is wanting to live.

LUCIA: While there are still masters, we haven't finished our mission.

SCHNEIDER: Days of action, days of creation,

LUCIA: Embrace your love without dropping your guard.

SCHNEIDER: I love you, Lucia.

LUCIA: Oh say it with bullets.

(A peace song breaks out across the camp; all the COMPANY move into the empty space, singing it – except for the TV CREW and the worker. The TV CREW start filming LUCIA and SCHNEIDER, who continue to lie across the entrance. A worker enters: it is the same man (the SECOND FIGURE) as in the Prologue. A jet begins to rev for take-off, momentarily drowning the song. The SECOND FIGURE takes the Second World War rifle from under his overcoat. He aims the rifle at the base. The jet screams. The peace song, very loud. A siren louder still.)